Opportunities in the Development of Pakistan's Private Sector

AUTHOR

Sadika Hameed

A Report of the CSIS Program on Crisis, Conflict, and Cooperation

September 2014

CSIS | CENTER FOR STRATEGIC & INTERNATIONAL STUDIES

ROWMAN & LITTLEFIELD

Lanham • Boulder • New York • Toronto • Plymouth, UK

About CSIS

For over 50 years, the Center for Strategic and International Studies (CSIS) has worked to develop solutions to the world's greatest policy challenges. Today, CSIS scholars are providing strategic insights and bipartisan policy solutions to help decisionmakers chart a course toward a better world.

CSIS is a nonprofit organization headquartered in Washington, D.C. The Center's 220 full-time staff and large network of affiliated scholars conduct research and analysis and develop policy initiatives that look into the future and anticipate change.

Founded at the height of the Cold War by David M. Abshire and Admiral Arleigh Burke, CSIS was dedicated to finding ways to sustain American prominence and prosperity as a force for good in the world. Since 1962, CSIS has become one of the world's preeminent international institutions focused on defense and security; regional stability; and transnational challenges ranging from energy and climate to global health and economic integration.

Former U.S. senator Sam Nunn has chaired the CSIS Board of Trustees since 1999. Former deputy secretary of defense John J. Hamre became the Center's president and chief executive officer in 2000.

CSIS does not take specific policy positions; accordingly, all views expressed herein should be understood to be solely those of the author(s).

ISBN: 978-1-4422-4030-8 (pb); 978-1-4422-4031-5 (eBook)

Center for Strategic & International Studies
1616 Rhode Island Avenue, NW
Washington, DC 20036
202-887-0200 | www.csis.org

Rowman & Littlefield
4501 Forbes Boulevard
Lanham, MD 20706
301-459-3366 | www.rowman.com

Contents

Acknowledgments

I would like to thank the Ploughshares Fund, whose generous contribution made this research possible. For all the assistance given during field research, I am also grateful to Mishal Pvt. Ltd. Pakistan, particularly Amir Jahangir, Asif Farouqi, Saleem Anwar, and Zahid Jaffery. I am especially grateful to Ayesha Shaukat who provided research assistance in Pakistan and helped find information to corroborate findings from the round tables and meetings. Lastly, I would like to thank the C3 team, and Raquel Gonzalez for research and editorial support. The content of this report represents my views only, not those of CSIS or any other institutions. Nothing in this report should be construed as offering investment advice. With the exception of a previous working relationship with Amir Jahangir, I do not have a financial stake in any company mentioned in this report.

1 | Introduction

Relations between the United States and Pakistan have begun to improve after several years of heightened tensions. Yet many challenges remain. Among them is how to improve Pakistan's economy. Its economic crisis is one of the main sources of its internal tensions, but multiple opportunities exist to improve its economic performance. The policy debate in the United States, however, is still dominated by a focus on terrorism and extremism. While Pakistan's stability is a natural concern for the United States, focusing primarily on security issues limits the options for improving stability.

Prior research by the CSIS Program on Crisis, Conflict, and Cooperation (C3) has found that U.S. engagement with and support for Pakistan's private sector holds a great deal of promise as a potential path to stability and as a more solid basis for a broader U.S.-Pakistan relationship beyond 2014. But while this fact is increasingly recognized, there has been little progress moving forward on such engagement.

This report present the results of a series of workshops, field research, and interviews to identify concrete opportunities for engaging with Pakistan's private sector, while benefiting the U.S. economy. While acknowledging that there are a number of risks to investment in Pakistan, it moves beyond the simple claim that less risky opportunities exist in Pakistan, seeking instead to identify where those opportunities lie. This chapter summarizes the issues at stake. The remainder of the report reviews sectors the author has identified as being ripe for potential investment in Pakistan, with discussions of opportunities that exist in the stock market, financial services, logistics, information and communication technologies (ICTs), agriculture, fast-moving consumer goods (FMCGs), pharmaceuticals, real estate, renewable and alternative energy, mining, low-cost private education, and retail. Appendix A provides pertinent economic facts and figures, including a breakdown by economic group of U.S. foreign direct investment (FDI) in Pakistan for the period from July 2011 through May 2012 (see Table A.1.). Appendix B offers a series of company profiles, mostly through interviews with founders or chief executive officers (CEOs), that stand as examples of the investment potential in Pakistan.

Background

Since the financial crisis of 2008, Pakistan has faced incredible security challenges and economic turbulence. However, it is also the first time a democratically elected government has been reelected and Pakistan stands as one of the "Next Eleven" economies[1] after the BRICS. Thus, as one Pakistani businessman put it in an interview with the author, "it has been the most turbulent yet exciting of times for Pakistani entrepreneurs."[2] One stabilizing hope lies with Pakistan's business community, which remains optimistic about Pakistan's economy outlook and about business focus of the Nawaz government.[3] If there is one thing that becomes clear when looking at a complex country like Pakistan, it is that where there are gaps there are also innumerable opportunities. Filling these gaps can be both highly profitable, while also providing a valuable boost to the Pakistani economy and its people by providing private-sector–led solutions to developmental problems. Or as Arif Naqvi, one of Pakistan's most prominent entrepreneurs, said, "If everyone says, 'Heck no!' there should be huge opportunities for arbitrage."[4]

When identifying opportunities for creating jobs and the potential for entrepreneurship, nobody says it better than Jump Start Pakistan:

> The only way you can generate wealth [in Pakistan] is through Entrepreneurship, but that is not the only aspect—more importantly you solve problems. There is a sizable population of Pakistan where malnutrition is alarmingly becoming a serious issue. These people have not been able to feed themselves and their families due to food inflation and lack of job opportunities. Rather than relying on governmental ideals or NGOs, *nobody has come forward with an entrepreneurial mindset* to come up with ideas to produce multivitamins for poor families, no one has suggested and sold tomato seeds to these families cheaply so they can grow tomato plants in their back yard and have a free supply of tomatoes into the next season when everyone will be selling them in market place at almost double the price of tomatoes sold in London. The options are abundant and clear to entrepreneurs who want to enrich Pakistan.[5]

Although Pakistan is still new on the scene when it comes to innovation and entrepreneurship, changes are happening quickly. Pakistan has been identified as a very viable country for profitmaking by institutional investors. Goldman Sachs has, since 2007, identified Pakistan as one of the Next Eleven after the BRICS.[6] Even in the face of uncertainty and the many other challenges Pakistan faces, companies are innovating, growing, and becoming far more resilient. As Anne Habiby, cofounder of AllWorld Network said, "Pakistanis on

---

1. Goldman Sachs identified the "Next 11" to be the countries that would be the next emerging markets, or have potential to become emerging markets.

2. Author interview with Amir Jahangir, CEO, Mishal Pvt. Ltd., Lahore, March 2014.

3. CSIS/Mishal Roundtables: Karachi, December 2013; Lahore, December 2013; Islamabad, January 2014.

4. Josh Lerner, Asim Ijaz Khwaja, and Ann Leamon, "Abraaj Capital and the Karachi Electric Supply Company," Case Study, Harvard Business School, February 9, 2012.

5. Italics added by the author. In the Jumpstart Pakistan model, CEOs of existing companies will take these new startups on board, provide them with a greenhouse environment in which they can organically grow, and be the new CEOs of the startups. The CEOs invest in exchange for equity. In the driving seat during the startup phase, they will train a cofounder to ultimately become the CEO, stepping down once the person is ready to assume the responsibility of chief executive. Jump Startup Pakistan, "What, why, how?," http://www.jumpstart pakistan.com/#what.

6. Goldman Sachs, "Beyond the BRICS: A look at the next 11," April 2007, http://www.goldmansachs.com /our-thinking/archive/archive-pdfs/brics-book/brics-chap-13.pdf.

the Arabia 500 are un-put-downable."[7] In fact, in 2011–2012, when U.S.-Pakistan relations were at their worst, Pakistan ranked number two on the Arabia fast growth 500.[8] Additionally, Pakistan is the ninth largest English-speaking nation in the world and the third largest in Asia, thereby removing the language barrier for doing business.

There are a number of other factors that have contributed to increased innovation and a move toward greater entrepreneurship. The innovation and entrepreneurial trend away from salaried jobs and the bias toward working for blue chip companies is changing because of young, forward-thinking individuals. First, many young people have studied in different countries and have been exposed to entrepreneurship and a Silicon Valley approach. Second, many of Pakistan's youth have had to create employment for themselves, as the financial crisis of 2008 triggered Pakistan's toughest economic years. And third, as the rupee devalued and savings were depleted many families who wished to send their children abroad to study were unable to do so. These youth went to some of the best universities in Pakistan and created a culture of entrepreneurship by capitalizing on local knowledge and foreign education taught in these institutions. For example, prior to 2008, there were very few business incubator (or incubator-like) programs within universities; as needs changed so too have the tools available to create an enabling environment for entrepreneurship.

What is particularly heartening (and also a sign of investor promise) is the number of Pakistanis abroad who are using Pakistan for backward integration because they also believe in paying it forward.[9] For example, the incubator Peshawar 2.0 categorically states in its road map that one objective is to "rebrand and rebuild Peshawar by harnessing cutting-edge technology, design and art."[10] Many Pakistanis with successful existing start-ups in Silicon Valley (for example JumpStart Pakistan and Atif Mumtaz's Personforce) are using their expertise in Pakistan now. While making profits, they are also making concerted efforts to transfer knowledge and technology.

---

7. Author interview with Nofel Daud, National Bank of Pakistan, Lahore, April 2014; author interview with Aqar Ahmed, Sustainable Development Policy Institute (SDPI), Islamabad, April 2014. "The 500s rigorously discover and credential a new breed of entrepreneurs with a track record of success in growth markets. This is the largest system to find entrepreneurs and bring them to world-wide attention—a system that thousands of market actors can leverage for growth, jobs and prosperity." AllWorld Network, "AllWorld Network Overview," http://www.allworldlive.com/about/overview.

8. "AllWorld was co-founded by Harvard Business School Professor Michael E. Porter, Deirdre M. Coyle Jr., and Anne S. Habiby. Its aim is to bring visibility to growing companies in emerging markets to increase their odds of success. Any private, non-listed company with rapid sales growth and an ability to demonstrate results with audited financial statements was invited to compete for a spot on the inaugural Arabia500." AllWorld Network, "Pakistan #2 on the Arabia Fast Growth 500: Pakistan breaks records as a hub for entrepreneurs," http://www.allworldlive.com/feed/press/pakistan-2-arabia-fast-growth-500-pakistan-breaks-records-hub -entrepreneurs. The Arabia 500 is an initiative of the AllWorld network of the fastest growing companies.

9. Backward integration is "a form of vertical integration that involves the purchase of suppliers. Companies will pursue backward integration when it will result in improved efficiency and cost savings. For example, backward integration might cut transportation costs, improve profit margins and make the firm more competitive. By way of contrast, forward integration is a type of vertical integration that involves the purchase or control of distributors." Investopedia, "Definition of backward integration," http://www.investopedia.com/terms/b/back wardintegration.asp.

10. Peshawar 2.0, "Road Map: Our means to the end," http://www.peshawar2.org/about-us/roadmap/.

Changes are on the horizon for many Pakistani businesses. Like many developing countries, Pakistan has a large number of businesses that are family owned and hesitant to part with part equity[11] stakes (ownership) to outsiders. However, much of the younger generation, which has been exposed to Western financial practices for growth, realize that financial models in Pakistan must change for businesses to grow and prosper. For example, one important change is the increased acceptance of alternative forms of financing, such as private equity and venture capital. Pakistan's experiences with private equity up to 2011 was not good. The market both in terms of supply and demand were not ready for such financing. Financial institutions struggled to sell it as a form of alternative financing and consumers were unwilling to enter into private equity deals. But as the entrepreneurial landscape changed, so too did the financial landscape. It is not just a change in thinking but also financial realities forcing these changes. The short-term T-bill[12] (which determines the interest rate for loans) is very high compared to many others at 10 percent.[13] For medium-sized investors, collateral and traditional-based lending is very expensive, given that the base rate is very high. Thus, entrepreneurs are now more open to lending with equity stakes, especially as the market matures with appropriate buy-back clauses and more sophisticated mechanisms to protect both investors and the recipients. Both demand and supply factors have influenced this change.

Furthermore, as corporate governance and corporate transparency are becoming more important, successful Pakistani entrepreneurs are also openly acknowledging the need for transparent practices.[14]

There are a number of important things to note and caveat in this report:

- Though investment and trade can never be divorced, this report focuses more on competitive sectors and the potential for investments. It focuses on the bottom line of both Pakistani and U.S. companies, while acknowledging that investments that create jobs and that liquidity will benefit Pakistan.

- After much research, this report has been narrowed to focus on U.S. and Pakistani medium-sized entrepreneurs.[15] In the case of the United States, large multinational companies (MNCs) or U.S.-based companies are already present in the Pakistani

---

11. Equity is a form of ownership interest in an enterprise.

12. A short-term T-bill is a government bond with a maturity of less than one year. Pakistan investment bonds (PIBs), a form of debt, are a way of raising money for the government. In Pakistan's case, PIBs are often used to service other debt coming due, particularly to multilateral institutions.

13. This in an opportunity for American investors because the short-term T-bill has a B rating according to Standard and Poor's. It does not require long-term risk exposure.

14. Ijaz Nasir, "100 business leaders, entrepreneurs and difference makers of Pakistan," *Manager Today*; author interview with Saqib Hamdani, CEO, TCS Pvt. Ltd.; author interview with Abrar Hasan, CEO, National Foods, Karachi, April 2014. For a comprehensive list of laws relating to foreign investments in different sectors, see KPMG, *Investment in Pakistan: An Introduction* (Karachi: KPMG, 2013), http://www.kpmg.com/PK/en/Issues AndInsights/ArticlesPublications/Documents/Investment-in-Pakistan2013.pdf.

15. It is true that the definition of "medium-sized" entrepreneurs differs for the two countries. However, this report will not restrict the definition across the board for either country because the metrics normally used (number of employees, revenues, tax revenues) differ across the sectors. It does not make sense to take one metric and definition and apply it across the board.

market and have the know-how to mitigate the risks in frontier markets.[16] As medium-sized entrepreneurs grow, they are looking to invest in frontier markets for market capitalization and access, which at the moment is difficult in the BRICS countries.[17] These entrepreneurs lack the risk exposure that larger entrepreneurs do. Also, on the Pakistani side, medium-sized entrepreneurs have a track record of success and more often than not have the requisite documentation for compliance, thus reducing the risk exposure and any violation of the Foreign Corrupt Practices Act (FCPA). After two years of interviews, this report focuses on (but is not restricted to) $1 million to $15 million investments. However, it is worth noting that since Pakistan is poised as one of the Next Eleven, the United States should consider additional preferential trade agreements. Most respondents felt that something similar to the GSP (Generalized System of Preferences) *plus* status given by the European Union to Pakistan could be beneficial for both countries.[18]

- The distinction between trade and investment has been made for another reason. It is possible for U.S. investors to invest in competitive sectors of Pakistan or enter into co-ventures even if the target market for the product is not in the United States. For example, although the United States has been one of the largest markets for Pakistan in the textile industry, future U.S. demands may not meet Pakistan's future production levels. However, investments in Pakistan's growing textile industry could benefit from sales in other markets, such as the United Arab Emirates or China.

- There are case studies in this report of successful entrepreneurs within the competitive sectors. First, these case studies are in *no* way an exhaustive list or even any kind of ranking of Pakistani entrepreneurs. The entrepreneurs were able to meet with the author during field visits to Lahore, Islamabad, and Karachi. Second, the case studies differ between each other because the research and interview formats evolved as the project progressed.

Also worth noting, though this report is focusing largely on investments, is that the goal is for these investments to be made while creating jobs for Pakistan's youth. A breakdown by sector of employment in Pakistan is shown in Appendix A (Table A.2.). Another factor that often gets overlooked is when investors review Pakistan's market capitalization, which is low, and do not take into account the informal/undocumented economy that is as large as the documented $250 billion economy.[19]

---

16. That said, all sectors identified here also have potential for large U.S. companies if they do want to penetrate or further invest in the Pakistani market.

17. As the BRICS countries face over heating of their economies, they prove too expensive a playing ground for medium-sized American entrepreneurs, who also face competition from larger U.S. or multinational companies.

18. Under the GSP plus agreement, approximately 20 percent of imports from Pakistan will be tax exempt. The remaining will be taxed on a preferential basis.

19. See the stock exchange discussion in Chapter 2 for efforts being made by the Pakistani government to formalize the informal economy via the stock exchange.

U.S. Interests in a Stable Pakistani Economy

Although investment waned between 2004 and 2012, Pakistan is on average the third largest recipient of foreign direct investment (FDI) in comparison with similar countries. The two largest recipients of comparable countries are Nigeria and Libya.[20] See Appendix A (Table A.3.) for total U.S. FDI and a comparison of FDI for seven East Asia countries between 2004 and 2012.

Recent budget cuts and sequestration in the United States have accelerated the move in development circles toward private-sector–led development. With less money to use for development projects, donors have been searching for a method to spark self-sustaining improvements in society. Increasingly, donors are working to enable businesses in developing countries to hire, produce, and grow. The emphasis on private-sector development offers particular promise in fragile or violence-affected states, where the private sector is often the only functioning institution in society and security threats limit access for outside officials.

These international development challenges are not only faced by the United States. More generally, the formula for calculating aid is being challenged. There are many cases where the official system determining whether the interest rate is low enough to qualify for official development assistance (ODA) has gone awry, resulting in aid being given that should instead be profitable loans.[21]

U.S. foreign assistance efforts in Pakistan currently depend on large infusions of money, with a blend of military aid, civilian development, relief programs, and direct budgetary support to encourage Pakistani cooperation with U.S. foreign policy objectives. This aid approach is funded by the Kerry-Lugar-Berman Bill, which will expire in 2014. Despite the 2014 troop drawdown in Afghanistan and drastic reductions in U.S. foreign aid for Pakistan, stability in Pakistan will remain a U.S. foreign policy priority. Pakistan's nuclear arsenal and militants especially will remain a concern for U.S. policymakers and will require U.S. involvement in the region despite constraints on resources and political will. Key components of U.S. strategy will be to reduce militancy, increase employment, and strengthen Pakistan's regional integration in an effort to stabilize the country without massive U.S. expenditures. As with fragile states around the world, stabilization and development efforts are likely to focus increasingly on developing the local private sector.

Efforts to stabilize Pakistan by strengthening the private sector and business involvement will depend first on addressing international perceptions of Pakistan. News coverage

---

20. Why Nigeria and Libya are the largest recipients of direct investment is beyond the scope of this report. It is worth noting, however, that both Nigeria and Libya have significant oil reserves; the investment numbers have not been segregated for non–oil-related investments.

21. David Roodman, "The Crisis in Official Development Assistance (ODA) Statistics: Needed Revamp Would Lift Japan, Lower France," Center for Global Development, June 2011, http://www.cgdev.org/blog/crisis -official-development-assistance-oda-statistics-needed-revamp-would-lift-japan-lower?utm_source=140610 &utm_medium=cgd_email&utm_campaign=cgd_weekly&utm_&&&.

and public attention to Pakistan center on the threats emanating from Pakistan as well as the strained relationship between the U.S. and Pakistani governments. This focus obscures the tremendous economic potential that Pakistan offers: 180 million consumers, a rapidly growing private sector, its location as a shipping hub, and one of the most favorable demographic age distributions in the world. Investment in Pakistan presents an area of shared interest for the Pakistani government, the U.S. government, the people of Pakistan, and business professionals in the United States. Average Pakistanis would see their economic livelihood improve. Businesses in both countries would see their bottom line improve. The U.S. government would be able to achieve its stabilization objectives without major expenditures.

Despite frequent depictions of Pakistan as dangerous and hostile, Pakistan possesses a number of desirable structural traits. The first is the age structure of Pakistan's population. Pakistan's enormous young population is often depicted as a threat to its stability, as young, unemployed people can become radicalized. Around 68 percent of Pakistan's population is regarded as youth. To absorb this youth bulge, Pakistan's real gross domestic product (GDP) needs to grow at an estimated annual average rate in excess of 7 percent.[22] A private-sector–led development approach turns the youth bulge from a liability into an asset. The youth bulge can be extremely promising from a business standpoint, creating a demographic dividend due to a high ratio of young workers versus retired people. Many observers credit China's demographic dividend for a portion of its incredible growth.

A second, and related, trend is the increase in Pakistani consumer spending. As Pakistan's young population moves into cities and ages into more prosperous late twenties and early thirties, Pakistan's demand for consumer goods will rapidly increase. This trend is already visible in Pakistan's 7.5 percent compounded annual growth rate in consumer spending since 2007. Nominal per capita income has grown by 3.5 percent in 2012–2013 to US$1,368.[23] Multinational corporations that operate in Pakistan, including Unilever, Colgate-Palmolive, and Nestle, have seen faster revenue growth in Pakistan than their global average.

Pakistan also presents opportunities for financial investment. A very low percentage of Pakistani small and medium enterprises (SMEs) have bank loans (7 percent).[24] Local companies have seen high growth (35 percent two-year median compound growth for the top-performing AllWorld Pakistan 100). Greater access to capital could increase the number of companies experiencing high growth and could deliver high returns for foreign investors. From a development perspective, SMEs are able to rapidly increase employment and their local ties ensure that they make local investments and continue operating, even in the face of security threats.

Foreign investors have another reason to invest in Pakistan. As Western investors seek to hedge against market changes, they seek to diversity investments into assets with low

---

22. Government of Pakistan, Planning Commission, *Pakistan: Framework for Economic Growth* (Islamabad: Planning Commission, May 2011), http://www.pc.gov.pk/hot%20links/growth_document_english_version.pdf.
23. KPMG, *Investment in Pakistan*.
24. This figure stands in contrast to 32 percent of SMEs in Bangladesh and 33 percent in India.

correlations with existing investments. Recent research has examined the potential of Africa to provide regional diversification through its low market correlations with the United States and Europe.[25] Research by Pakistani economists indicates that the market correlation with Pakistan is even lower (around 0.05).[26] With a market capitalization equivalent to Nigeria, the Karachi Stock Exchange (KSE) can absorb foreign investment, and its low price-to-earnings ratio brings greater dividends at lower cost.

All of these factors are latent in Pakistan and provide an impetus for international investment and the raw material for local business to grow. The U.S. government could, with minimal expenditure, lift many of the barriers to inclusive, private-sector-led growth in Pakistan while benefiting the U.S. economy as well.

Many local companies prioritize infrastructure, better regulation, and lower corruption over increased FDI, making U.S. investments in technical assistance profitable.[27] U.S. policy in fragile states addresses these objectives already. Better coordination between the U.S. embassy, U.S. businesses, and local companies can help target U.S. development work toward specific undertakings that will promote local economic growth.[28] These three policy changes can redirect shrinking aid and diminishing attention toward the sectors of Pakistan where they will have the longest impact. In a number of the sectors identified, there is already wealth and money available locally that needs help to be channeled into viable projects; American investment can reap returns by partnering with Pakistani organizations.[29]

Lastly, Pakistani entrepreneurs can help mitigate risks for foreign companies. Through co-ventures, they can enter markets with large potentials without compromising quality or ethics. An example of this is the partnership that DHL has with a Pakistani company called TCS; cooperation began in 1983, when Pakistani was not as open an economy as it is now and was also under military rule.[30] Due to strict regulations, the government of Pakistan wanted the local partner (TCS) to restrict operations to international courier services (to narrow foreign exchange liability) in exchange for complete repatriation of profits. The Pakistani government also wanted TCS to be fully responsible for any security violations. For this venture to be successful, TCS would need to have operational control over DHL in Pakistan. In order to capture the market and also ensure quality, DHL undertook training

25. Todd Moss and Ross Thuotte, "Nowhere Left to Hide? Stock Market Correlation, Regional Diversification, and the Case for Investing in Africa," Working Paper 316, Center for Global Development, March 2013, http://www.cgdev.org/sites/default/files/1427009_file_Moss_Thuotte_market_correlations_FINAL.pdf.

26. Kashif Hamid and Arshad Hasan, "Casual and Dynamic Linkage of Stock Markets: An Empirical Study of Karachi Stock Exchange (KSE) with Emerging and Developed Equity Markets," *African Journal of Business Management* 5, no. 19 (September 9, 2011): 7802–7817.

27. John Bray, "The role of private sector actors in post-conflict recovery," *Conflict, Security & Development* 9, no. 1 (April 2009).

28. Sadika Hameed and Kathryn Mixon, *Private-Sector Development in Fragile, Conflict-Affected, and Violent Countries* (Washington, DC: CSIS, July 2013), http://csis.org/files/publication/130617_Hameed_PrivateSecDevel_WEB.pdf.

29. Author interview with Rumman Ahmed, CEO, Dynasty, Karachi, April 2014.

30. TCS is not just a case study in this report but is in fact also a Harvard Business School case study of success and a case study in one of Philip Kotler's books on marketing. See Philip Kotler and Gary Armstrong, *Principles of Marketing*, 13th ed. (Saddle River, NJ: Prentice Hall, 2010).

operations of key personnel and in the following years DHL Pakistan outperformed counterparts in the region.[31]

U.S. strategic and business interests do not necessarily differ. As a sign of confidence in Pakistan's competitive sectors, the Overseas Private Investment Corporation (OPIC) has invested large amounts into these sectors. OPIC has worked with a wide variety of projects and sectors in Pakistan including health care, telecommunications, energy, construction, finance, and microfinance. Recent projects in Pakistan include medical health care facility expansion, expansion of mobile telecommunications infrastructure, and development of a new biomass power plant.[32] A comprehensive list of OPIC investments in Pakistan is given in Appendix A (Table A.4.).

Methodology

A number of steps were taken for this research. First, the author conducted consultations in both Pakistan and the United States for two years about the feasibility of Pakistan as both a frontier market for investment and its strategic importance. Second, the CSIS team reviewed published literature to examine what had already been written and tried. Third, roundtables were held in Washington D.C., Lahore, Islamabad, and Karachi with individuals from government, the private sector, civil society, representatives of business chambers and associations, and other policymakers. Fourth, these roundtables were supplemented with 92 individual interviews. The results in this report are the interpretation and analysis of the author alone and are not the views of any individual or CSIS. A number of case studies are presented in Appendix B to give examples of the types of Pakistani firms that could be viable partners to help mitigate community and political risk for American investors. These cases are *not* an exhaustive list of viable partners.

---

31. Walter Kuemmerle and Zahid Ahmed, "TCS: An Entrepreneurial Air-Express Company in Pakistan," Case Study, Harvard Business School, April 22, 2004.
32. Overseas Private Investment Corporation (OPIC), *OPIC 2012 Annual Report: Building for Growth, Innovating for Change* (Washington, DC: OPIC, 2012), http://www.opic.gov/sites/default/files/files/OPIC_2012_Final.pdf.

2 | Competitive Sectors and Areas for Investment

The risks in Pakistan are well known and, in some respects, overblown. Certainly there are issues with security, red tape, and corruption, as well as a number of market failures, as discussed in the previous chapter. But this chapter highlights Pakistan's competitive sectors, those that are ripe for growth and where American investment would have a strategic advantage. For a snapshot of sectors where U.S. foreign direct investment (FDI) already flows in Pakistan, see Appendix A (Table A.1.).

The Stock Market

Returns on stocks traded in the Karachi Stock Exchange (KSE) grew by 50 percent between 2012 and 2013. The KSE 100 Index rose by 200 percent during the three years ending in 2013. In fact in the first half of 2013, KSE grew 40 percent, outperforming every stock market except Japan that the *Economist* tracks. Of the top 100 best-performing equity funds in the world in 2012, 14 were Pakistani. Karachi-based Safeway Mutual Fund, for example, ranked as the 18th best-performing fund with a 74 percent return that year.[1] (See Appendix B for case studies for AKD Securities Ltd., Safeway Fund Ltd., and IQ Ventures.) The impressive returns are due in part to an amnesty scheme, implemented between January 2012 and June 2014, whereby the Pakistani government permitted investors to purchase shares without demonstrating where the money had come from as a way to encourage entry into the formal economy. It was due as well, however, to growing investor confidence, particularly after the successful election of May 2013. Volatility, and therefore risk, is fairly high, but returns have very low correlations with Western stock exchanges, so some investors put money into KSE-listed stocks to diversify their portfolios.[2]

Returns on the short-term bond is particularly high. The interest rate on Pakistan's short-term T-bill is 10 percent and has a Standard and Poor's (S&P) risk rating of B (the same as Indonesia and Vietnam). The risk rating for the long-term T-bill is B minus.

---

1. Nishant Kumar, "42 Asian equity funds among world's top 100 in 2012—Lipper," Reuters, January 22, 2013, http://www.reuters.com/article/2013/01/23/asia-equityfunds-rank-idUSL4N0AM5SH20130123.

2. In January 2012, the government of Pakistan declared that investors could buy shares with no questions asked about the origination of the money. The amnesty will last until June 2014. The purpose was to encourage people to invest their undocumented funds in the market, thus becoming part of the documented formal economy. "How did Karachi get a world-beating stock exchange?," *Economist*, July 28, 2013, http://www.economist.com/blogs/economist-explains/2013/07/economist-explains-19.

Increasing investor confidence and participation in the stock exchange is a positive trend for the future. As the BRICS economies heat up, investors will continue to look toward frontier markets, particularly the Next Eleven, which includes Pakistan.

While previously the trading of T-bills was restricted to institutional investors, the opening up of the secondary bond market will result in three things. First, trading generally will increase, allowing greater capital flows into the market. Second, T-bills can be purchased by non-institutional investors, thus forcing increased competitiveness and efficiency while also providing greater yields. Third, as the stock market matures, with increased market capitalization and liquidity flows, it is expected that more sophisticated financial instruments, such as different types of derivatives, will develop, allowing for greater hedging strategies.

The Securities and Exchange Commission of Pakistan (SECP) allows individuals and companies to own 100 percent of the shares of a company. The main draw for foreign and American investors is that all income after taxes are remittable, removing long-term political risk of assets in the country.[3] As one investor put it, "The best time to invest in a country is often when its economy is emerging from recession and all of the bad news is in the rear view mirror."[4] (Also see IQ Ventures case study in Appendix B.)

Financial Services
PRIVATE EQUITY AND VENTURE CAPITAL

Pakistan's experience (as noted earlier) in private equity prior to 2011 was rocky, given that Pakistani entrepreneurs did not have the knowledge of such lending. Investment firms and brokerage houses faced immense challenges in selling this as an alternative form of financing. However, this is set to change for a number of reasons. First, as traditional collateral-based lending has become more difficult, there is more demand for alternative forms of financing, such as revenue-based lending. Second, Pakistani financial markets are evolving (see AKD Securities and Safeway Fund case studies in Appendix B) and becoming more sophisticated. Third, there has been a shift in thinking among youth and family-owned businesses toward a greater acceptance of equity-based lending. There are a number of brokerage houses and investment banks that help broker equity deals. Interestingly, even incubation centers such as the newly created LUMS (Lahore University of Management Sciences) Center for Entrepreneurship will also be taking direct equity stakes in entrepreneurs that enter their program, creating greater efficiencies on both sides.[5] At the moment there are few investment banks or brokerage houses that take direct equity stakes in businesses with some exceptions, such as J.S. Bank (Jahangir

---

3. Farrukh Zafar, "Why and how KSE became the world's second-best performing market this year," *Express Tribune* (Karachi), October 6, 2013, http://tribune.com.pk/story/614407/record-making-why-and-how -kse-became-the-worlds-second-best-performing-market-this-year/.

4. Kyle Caldwell, "The 10 best performing stock markets of 2013," *Telegraph* (London), December, 2013, http://www.telegraph.co.uk/finance/personalfinance/investing/shares/10523334/The-10-best-performing-stock -markets-of-2013.html.

5. The Lahore University of Management Sciences is Pakistan's most famous university for social sciences. The business school was set up by top businessmen in Pakistan.

Siddiqui Bank). However, there are new players entering the market and older players that are expanding operations. (See the "Financial Services" case studies in Appendix B.)

There are no formal private equity or venture capital firms in their own right (they are usually a part of operations in banks and brokerage houses), but this is likely to change as entrepreneurship and demand for these financial services increases. Venture capital is very new for the Pakistani market. The increase in successful incubation centers has led thought leaders (including academics, government, leading business men and civil society) who have created incubation centers to increase their mandate to help entrepreneurs raise money through venture capital. For example, the company Xgear raised a US$40,000 nonequity seed fund using Indigogo an internet-based firm for crowd source funding.

Also, new young entrepreneurs are entering the financial markets and bringing change.[6] Currently, Pakistan lacks regulation for venture capital (VC) funds, which in fact face double taxation.[7] However, the SECP is increasingly coming under pressure to create regulation that is more investor friendly. Going forward, U.S. businesses can provide advice for creating the regulation and then implementing it for Pakistani businesses. While the Pakistani government's Qarza scheme is not a venture capital initiative per se, financiers are using this government initiative as an example of why the government should do everything possible for VC funds.[8] Nawaz Sharif, prime minister of Pakistan, announced the launch of the Qarza scheme in December 2013 for entrepreneurs between the ages of 21 and 45, with a 50 percent quota for women. While lending institutions usually will, at a minimum, lend to these individuals at 15 percent annually, the Qarza scheme lends at 8 percent. The total value of this initiative is Rs 100 billion for 100,000 loans. The maximum loan amount is Rs 2 million.[9]

The U.S. Agency for International Development (USAID) has recognized two things. First, that private-sector–led development is key; second, and as a result of the first, there is a strong potential for private equity. USAID has recently launched a private equity fund through the Pakistan Private Investment Initiative (PPII). At the time of writing this report, two of the three recipients had been announced—Abraaj Group and JS Private Equity Management (two of the most renowned names in private equity in Pakistan)—to increase private equity as a form of financing for small to medium-sized entrepreneurs. Both recipients received US$24 million and will commit to matching or exceeding this seed funding. The pooled funds are initially expected to be US$100 million.[10]

---

6. See case studies on Nihal Cassim's Safeway Fund Ltd. and Salman Haider Sheikh's I.Q. Ventures in Appendix B.

7. The double taxation issue is a very technical issue that goes beyond the scope of this report. However, it is worth noting that there is immense pressure on the SECP to develop regulations and remove barriers for VC funds such as double taxation.

8. "Qarza" literally means loan.

9. While the Qarza scheme has seen some successes it is still too new to gauge its viability. It is also facing challenges, particularly because the loan is not given to the individual but to a guarantor in many cases. See Irfan Haider, "Tough conditions keep youth from PM's loan scheme," *Dawn*, May 25, 2014, http://www.dawn .com/news/1108438.

10. USAID, "USAID launches private investment initiative to mobilize at least $150 million private equity investment," press release, June 25, 2013, http://www.usaid.gov/news-information/press-releases/usaid-partners -abraaj-and-jspe-150-million-private-equity-pakistan.

U.S. investors face two different types of opportunities. Though the PPII is an aid initiative, it gives an example of how partnering with private equity firms in Pakistan can mitigate risks. USAID administrator Rajiv Shah explained, "By partnering with Abraaj and JS Private Equity Management, USAID capitalizes on these companies' expertise to make smart investment decisions that will grow the Pakistani economy, create jobs, and generate profits for investors who seize the economic opportunities that Pakistan presents."[11] The second opportunity is that U.S. companies can enter into direct private equity investments in Pakistani enterprises. The incubation centers, partnered with some of Pakistan's top business schools, will be great repositories of information for viable entrepreneurs to make informed decisions about investing in venture capital or private equity.

MOBILE BANKING

The Pakistani government is aggressively trying to find alternative pathways to financial access and to formalize the economy by working with the 89 percent of the population that does not have bank accounts. Because 69 percent of Pakistanis use mobile phones, mobile banking is increasing. Although relatively new; branchless banking was first used in 2008. As a recent report from the Consultative Group to Assist the Poor (CGAP) says, "Pakistan is one of the fastest developing markets for branchless banking in the world. Clear regulations and a regulator that is willing to both listen to the private sector and provide incentives for innovation have promoted a dynamic branchless banking sector."[12] A study commissioned by Telenor to the Boston Consulting Group found that with the current trajectory, mobile financial services may increase financial inclusion in Pakistan by 20 percent, and lead to an increase in GDP of up to 3 percent by 2020.[13]

The State Bank of Pakistan (SBP) has issued a number of branchless banking licenses. Some of these banks have paired up with mobile phone companies to provide mobile banking. One such initiative is Easypaisa,[14] which is a joint collaboration between Telenor Pakistan and Tameer Microfinance Bank. Through their mobile phones and Easypaisa, Pakistanis can open a mobile bank account, transfer money, pay bills, and earn interest on savings. There are 22,000 outlets in 750 Pakistani cities where Easypaisa is accepted for the immediate processing and payment of bills; the customer provides the bill and the payment is processed immediately. Up to 5 million users use Easypaisa every month and approximately "117 million transactions worth over Rs 261 billion have been carried out through Easypaisa since [its] launch."[15] As Pakistan gears up for 3G and 4G mobile networks, demand for m-commerce (mobile commerce) will increase. There are currently few players in the mobile banking field, making it a good investment opportunity.

---

11. Ibid.
12. Chris Bold, "Branchless Banking in Pakistan: A Laboratory for Innovation," Consultative Group to Assist the Poor (CGAP), October 1, 2011, http://beta.cgap.org/publications/branchless-banking-pakistan-laboratory -innovation.
13. Telenor Group, "Easypaisa—banking services made easy," May 15, 2013, http://www.telenor.com/sustain ability/initiatives-worldwide/easypaisa-banking-services-made-easy/.
14. "Easypaisa" literally means easy money.
15. Telenor Group, "Easypaisa—banking services made easy."

Logistics

One of Pakistan's main draws is its geographical accessibility. Its location can provide vital air, sea, and land routes for many different countries. Many interviewees argued that U.S. demand for logistics related to the ongoing effort in Afghanistan has disproportionately driven the market, and that after the withdrawal the demand for these services will decrease. Although U.S. military demand may decrease, trends indicate that this is not true for the entire logistics market. First, as Pakistan and India continue to engage on trade, transit of goods through Pakistan will increase. Second, as countries in Asia try to increase trade with Central Asia, Pakistan is a natural conduit. Third, Pakistan itself is seeking to increase trade (and hence the associated market of logistics) with regional and international partners, particularly the Middle East, Central Asia, and North Africa. Fourth, as Pakistan's own industries grow, logistics will be a vital ancillary industry, without which other sectors will not be able to expand.[16]

Business Incubation Ventures

Almost all entrepreneurs identified that even more than investments in their ventures, they wanted to learn from American entrepreneurs more about moving up the value chain, improving quality of products and procedures through technology transfers, and direct mentoring. U.S. investors have two choices. First, they can start their own incubators in niche areas of expertise. Second, they can co-venture with existing incubator-type programs in academic institutions such as the Center for Entrepreneurship at the Lahore University of Management Sciences (LUMS), the MIT Enterprise Forum, and so on. Other than profit potential for U.S. investors by providing technical assistance, these incubators can also be used to find viable partners to do business with.

Pakistani entrepreneurs have responded well to incubator-type programs; many have gone on to become successful business people, winning awards for their innovation. (See the Alternate Solutions case study in Appendix B.)

Information and Communications Technologies

Information and communications technologies (ICTs) refers to the newer technologies of computers, the Internet, and phones and also incorporates media such as radio and television, due to their roles in the transmission of information.[17] Every individual interviewed by the author pointed out the ICT sector and its various components as areas of high potential for investment, joint ventures, and outsourcing. Participants in the roundtables pointed out that technology transfers that are government to government and business to business (B2B) should be explored because they have profit potential and could have massive

---

16. For examples of successful entrepreneurs, see case studies in Appendix B on TCS Pvt. Ltd. and e2e Solutions.

17. State Bank of Pakistan, "The State of Pakistan's Economy: The Role of ICTs in Growth and Poverty Alleviation," 2012, http://www.sbp.org.pk/reports/quarterly/fy07/first/special_section_2.pdf.

positive spillovers. Pakistan's ICT sector caters to almost all segments of the market, including hardware, software development, and mobile and web app development. In 2011 Pakistan ranked 28th globally in terms of attractiveness for co-ventures and investments in ICT structure (particularly because of the sophisticated infrastructure present); it ranked fourth in terms of financial attractiveness as an outsourcing destination.[18]

WHY IS THE GOVERNMENT OF PAKISTAN FOCUSING ON ICTS?

ICT and its applications have become a reality, having powerful and direct impacts on achieving specific economic and development goals in Pakistan.[19] ICTs play a major role in facilitating education by making accessible and available information resources from around the world in a matter of seconds.[20] Current world economic growth is primarily driven by innovation processes, value chains, and business models linked to ICTs. Additionally, ICTs can enhance poor people's opportunities by improving their access to markets, health care, and various government services.[21]

Transformation to ICT is effectively making digital literacy a prerequisite for both wage employment and creating one's own business. As Pakistan's window to capitalize on the demographic dividend narrows, so does the time frame to increase Pakistan's literacy rates. The traditional educational system should not be ignored. However, vocational training for entrepreneurship is now also a necessity. The fastest and cheapest way to reach the segment of society that needs the most help with skills development is through ICTs. ICT literacy not only qualifies people for jobs in conventional sectors, but also opens doors to participate in rapidly growing markets such as business process outsourcing and microwork.[22]

A study shows that ICT brings a positive impact on the education sector of Pakistan. Students agree that the usage of ICT improves their knowledge skills and helps in delivering better results. Availability and usage of ICT is essential to improving the educational efficiency of students. This indicates that availability of ICT in education is supportive for the students to improve their learning skills. The latest technologies of ICT are helpful for the students to better prepare their assignments and projects. The more availability and usage of ICT in the education sector, the more efficient students will be.[23]

The government of Pakistan is working to improve ease of business, viable exit strategies, and a transparent regulatory framework in the ICT sector. For example, all software and

---

18. KPMG, *Investment in Pakistan.*
19. Yusuf Haroon Mujahid, "Digital Opportunity Initiative for Pakistan: A paper evaluating Pakistani eReadiness initiative," n.d., http://unpan1.un.org/intradoc/groups/public/documents/apcity/unpan005832.pdf.
20. Joseph Wilson "ICT Sector Performance Review for Pakistan," draft, LIRNEasia, April 2011, http://lirn easia.net/wp-content/uploads/2010/07/PK_Draft_Telecom_Report_110411_Pakistan1.pdf.
21. State Bank of Pakistan, "The State of Pakistan's Economy."
22. International Telecommunication Union (ITU), *Digital Opportunities: Innovative ICT Solutions for Youth Employment* (Geneva: ITU, February 2014), http://www.itu.int/en/ITU-D/Digital-Inclusion/Youth-and-Children /Documents/YouthReport_2014.pdf.
23. M. Wasif Nisar, Ehsan Ullah Munir, and Shafqat Ali Shad, "Usage and Impact of ICT in Education Sector: A Study of Pakistan," *Australian Journal of Basic and Applied Sciences* 5, no. 12 (2011): 578–583, http://arxiv.org/pdf /1206.5132.pdf.

Internet-based businesses in Pakistan are exempt from income tax until 2016. Furthermore, foreign investors are allowed 100 percent equity stakes and can repatriate all profits until 2016. Information technology (IT) exports are also tax exempt until 2016. The ICT industry in Pakistan has faced increased liberalization, greater private-sector participation, enhanced competition in new technologies, lower prices, and better customer service.[24]

The government has also set up a number of "IT parks" and incubators to digitize and leverage the economy. They leverage ICTs for jobs, increase vocational training, and use technology to spur growth in the education and health sectors. For example, in August 2012, the Punjab Information Technology Board (PITB) launched Plan9, Pakistan's most innovative (and largest) government supported tech incubator. This initiative supports entrepreneurs in the "refinement of business plans, mentoring on product development, connecting with potential clients, advising on internal operations, affixing with domain-specific mentors and safeguarding legal concerns."[25] Many entrepreneurs interviewed by the author believe that Plan9 is a good incubator system because it builds in all relevant stakeholders and leverages their expertise and outreach as well.

Similarly, there are also academic and civil society–led incubation programs. Local entrepreneurs launched Peshawar 2.0, which promotes a problem-solving, can-do attitude through projects ranging from curriculum development, talks with successful entrepreneurs, and seminars for problem solving. The idea is to provide a platform for young innovators from all disciplines. Peshawar 2.0 provides local startups with all their needs, "from product design, branding and business models to fundraising and customer development through our local and global network of mentors, angels and advisers."[26]

Additionally, there are Pakistani entrepreneurs who serve the U.S. market through backward integration. They can be approached to help bridge information and knowledge gaps about investing in Pakistan. One such case is Atif Mumtaz and his company Personforce (see case study in Appendix B). Additionally, there are entrepreneurs that provide software, mobile apps, and web apps globally. (For examples, see the Creative Chaos and VisTech Solutions case studies in Appendix B.)

Pakistan also has successful entrepreneurs on the hardware side. For example, Nayatel has introduced fiber optics to the Pakistani market, despite facing stiff competition from international competitors with greater capital and technological know-how (see the case study in Appendix B).

ICTS AND THE INFORMATION GAP

One thing is clear from the interviews and roundtables: there is a significant information gap that increases risks for both investors and businesses. For U.S. businesses, the opportunities in Pakistan and the associated risks are unknown. Pakistani entrepreneurs recognized

---

24. Wilson, "ICT Sector Performance Review for Pakistan."
25. Plan9, "What Is Plan9?," http://plan9.pitb.gov.pk/about_us/what_is_plan9.
26. Peshawar 2.0, "Road Map: Our means to the end."

three things. First, in many cases they were unsure of the needs of U.S. businesses and foreign opportunities for corporate and joint-ventures. Second, they face a knowledge gap within Pakistan itself, for example, for job opportunities and to find skilled labor. Third, the United States has technologies and the experience for leveraging information and building information repositories.

In a recent CSIS study, entrepreneurs had identified the trade consulates in embassies as potentially being very viable in providing on the ground information about opportunities and local regulatory frameworks.[27] Such an initiative would certainly be welcome but there are also opportunities to co-venture with Pakistani businesses to identify these opportunities.

At least two entrepreneurs tried to address the information gap; they have done very well for themselves. Rozee.pk was started by Monis Rahman after working for 10 years in Silicon Valley. The idea behind Rozee.pk was to build Pakistan's first online recruitment portal. In 2008 Rozee.pk became one of Pakistan's first startups to raise venture capital funds from Silicon Valley.[28] *Forbes* magazine recently placed Monis Rahman number six on its list of "Ten Big Hitting Asian Businessmen under 50."[29]

> Today, Rozee.pk is used by 54,000 employers and 16 million professionals in Pakistan—over 40,000 job applications are processed through its servers each day. Prestigious organizations including the United Nations, Engro and MCB Bank use its software to power their online recruitment strategy. Rozee.pk has grown its revenues 8,500% since 2007, receiving the Pakistan Fast Growth 25 award as one of the country's fastest growing private companies from All World Network, affiliated with eminent Harvard University professor Michael Porter.[30]

Rozee.pk recently went international after the acquisition of the Saudi recruitment portal, Mihnati.com.[31]

The second entrepreneur is Rehan Shoukat, who is in the textile and sugar business. When he entered into business he found that there was no information available about raw cotton trading in Pakistan. For example, he could not find out who buys what, when, and at which part of the value chain.[32] There was no point of service information with buyers or textile players to know what is happening in the Pakistani market (with a few exceptions). For his own business he developed a research department at his company. Few people in the market knew about cotton research (if there were any, they were very expensive to

---

27. Sadika Hameed and Kathryn Mixon, "Private Sector Development in fragile, conflict-affected and violent countries," Center for Strategic and International Studies, June 2013, http://csis.org/publication/private-sector-development-fragile-conflict-affected-and-violent-countries.
28. Draper Fisher Jurvetson and ePlanet Capital (the same VCs that backed Hotmail and Skype).
29. Forbes, "Ten Big Hitting Asian Businessmen under 50," http://www.forbes.com/pictures/mim45gfje/monis-rahman/.
30. "Rozee.pk takes its success story global," *Blue Chip Magazine*, July 22, 2013, http://bluechipmag.com/rozee-pk-takes-its-success-story-global/.
31. Ibid.
32. The majority of cotton trade in Pakistan is directly linked to New York Stock Futures.

hire), so he hired fresh college graduates to set up a databank on cotton. Initially it was difficult but things got better. The databank/ data center is the backbone of his company even today. Other investors can benefit from this data repository now through a website— Pakistan Agriculture Research (par.com.pk). It provides data-based services about agriculture products to clients internationally.

ICTS AND SERVICES PROVISION IN EDUCATION

Increasing investments and co-ventures in incubator-type programs within academia can start from a young age. The cheapest (yet most profitable for U.S. businesses) way to do this is through technology transfers and transfers of knowledge from U.S. businesses. Pakistanis running such incubators, or entrepreneurs who are entering such incubation mechanisms, are willing to pay for technology that will, first, help them learn, and, second, also help them grow to be successful entrepreneurs. This will also pave the way for U.S. entrepreneurs to find viable partners in the Pakistani market. Such investments and co-ventures will not increase jobs directly because such programs focus on individuals. It is the products of these entrepreneurs and growth of their businesses that will increase employment. For example, entrepreneurs who work in the social sectors improve living standards, while making profits and hiring workers.

As mentioned earlier, Pakistan is facing a literacy crisis, coupled with high unemployment. Service providers, both public and private, are willing to pay to increase the amount and the quality of their services, particularly in education and health. Because these services are demand driven, U.S. businesses can benefit first from selling ICTs to education and health vendors, while also selling to target markets directly.

Agriculture and Agri-Based Businesses

Pakistan's economy is heavily dependent on agriculture. The agricultural sector accounts for 22 percent of national GDP. The agricultural market is constrained by poor functioning primary product markets and constrained access to assets. Additionally, distribution of land and benefits is highly distorted and unequal. About 2 percent of the households control more than 45 percent of the land area.[33] Agriculture credit schemes typically benefit the larger farmers. However, there are positive trends as well as some opportunities for investment and co-ventures.

DAIRY

Pakistan is the fourth largest producer of milk in the world, yet the market remains highly fragmented primarily because of scattered and small dairy farms and the absence of cool chains and cold storage. Large multinational companies such as Nestle have been able to

---

33. World Bank, "Pakistan: Priorities for Agriculture and Rural Development," http://web.worldbank.org /WBSITE/EXTERNAL/COUNTRIES/SOUTHASIAEXT/EXTSAREGTOPAGRI/0,,contentMDK:20273773~menuPK:548216 ~pagePK:34004173~piPK:34003707~theSitePK:452766,00.html.

successfully bring together suppliers in this highly fragmented market. Similarly, Pakistani businesses such as National Foods and Gourmet have also been able to achieve success and are looking to expand operations into other countries or enter into the supply chains of foreign companies.

People interviewed and roundtable participants identified two main areas where U.S. investment would have a strategic advantage. First, U.S. investments could assist Pakistani companies with cool chains and cold storage to address the issue of fragmentation in the dairy sector. Pakistan itself is a large market, but as the logistics sector grows, the potential to service other markets will increase. From government perspectives, as future food security comes more to the forefront this is an important avenue to consider. Second, U.S. investors could assist Pakistani dairy farmers with technical help, such as the expertise to move up the value chain and into dairy-related products such as cheese.

It is worth noting that the ancillary market of halal meat will be targeted for expansion and exports by players in the Middle East and North Africa. Over time these businesses are looking to also enter the halal meat market in Western economies. The success of businesses such as Gourmet, K&N Chicken, National Foods, and Shan Foods domestically and their track record of expanding into other countries make them viable business partners for U.S. investors.

CORPORATE FARMING

At the moment, with falling yields, the inability to engage in crop rotation, and price volatility, the future for small farmers appears bleak. If not regulated properly, corporate farming can actually result in what is viewed as land grabbing and losses for small farmers. Currently, farmers are subsidized by the government; going forward, as the Pakistani government faces immense macroeconomic pressures, increased subsidies will be unaffordable. Small farmers face challenges of actual farming processes and, because of Pakistan's complex farm to market systems, with middlemen charging farmers to allow produce into the wholesale markets.[34]

Because subsidies are not a sustainable strategy, the government is seeking alternatives. Corporate farming provides the solutions—if handled correctly—to bring together small farmers and cut out the rent-seeking agents. Corporate farming also has overcome the problems of produce going from farm to market, particularly the challenges presented by high rents charged at each stage of production by different agents.

U.S. investments that would have a strategic advantage would involve mechanization of farm to market procedures, co-ventures with companies such as e2e Solutions (see case study in Appendix B) who are looking to expand into corporate farming and already have the technical experience, and investments in cold storage. Corporate farming ventures such as Engro Foods and Nestle received approximately 25 percent ROE on average.[35]

---

34. The actual farm to market systems are complex and beyond the scope of this report.
35. Presentation by Future Pakistan Business Today, "Investment opportunities in Pakistan." Hard (print) copy provided to author.

Fast-Moving Consumer Goods

Fast-moving consumer goods (FMCGs) are low-cost, non-durable consumables such as processed foods, toys, toiletries, salt, cooking oil, tea, and other essentials (including, in some definitions, fast-food products). As Pakistan's population grows, so does the need for basic necessities.[36] A number of Pakistani and multinational companies supply FMCGs to the Pakistani market to meet that demand, and some Pakistani firms have been successful enough that they have expanded into other markets.[37] Demand for generic FMCGs has been growing, and it is widely believed that there is pent-up demand for recognized brand names as well.[38] There was almost unanimous consensus from the interviews, roundtables, and independent research that there is immense potential for American investment in the FMCG sector. The Pakistani market has responded very favorably to foreign brands such as Nestle, Colgate-Palmolive, Proctor and Gamble, Unilever, and Johnson & Johnson. Food franchises such as McDonalds and Burger King are doing very well in Pakistan. The typical growth rates for branded food products are about 15 to 25 percent annually and the total food market each year grows by approximately 10 percent.[39] The National Foods case study (see Appendix B) is an example of local entrepreneurs capitalizing on Pakistan's FMCG market and expanding into other markets.

Pharmaceuticals

Over the past 20 years, Pakistan's pharmaceutical industry has improved basic infrastructure. There are approximately 600 pharmaceutical companies operating in Pakistan. The share of national companies is increasing with about 20 percent of the domestic need covered internally.[40] The local pharmaceutical industry ensures that the country has the capacity to support many domestic needs. In 2012, over $400 million of medicine was exported.[41]

Initially, the entire requirements for pharmaceuticals and drugs was met through imports. Population growth, increased urbanization, and provision of medical coverage to the growing number of government employees resulted in increased demand for products and the expansion of the industry. Furthermore, as Pakistani businesses generally grow

---

36. See case study on I.Q. Ventures in Appendix B.

37. See case study on National Foods in Appendix B.

38. Many American-based MNCs such as Nestle, Colgate-Palmolive, Unilever, and so on are already present in the Pakistani market. However, these are large sized companies with the risk exposure and the experience to navigate Pakistan's somewhat complicated regulatory environment, unlike medium sized entrepreneurs.

39. Author interview of Abrar Hasan, CEO, National Foods, Karachi, April 2014.

40. Mohammad Amir and Khalid Zaman, "Review of Pakistan Pharmaceutical Industry: SWOT Analysis, 2011" *International Journal of Business and Information Technology* 1, no. 1 (June 2011), http://www.google .com/url?sa=t&rct=j&q=&esrc=s&source=web&cd=1&ved=0CB8QFjAA&url=http%3A%2F%2Fwww.ojs.exceling-tech.co.uk%2Findex.php%2FIJBIT%2Farticle%2Fdownload%2F30%2F13&ei=VmrNU6DUPI62yASZtoLQDA&usg =AFQjCNFVPUVzBAOkOBJQxZ7cA1rs8lC6MA&sig2=Qf93Tgsj06ZHRtyfo91PQA&bvm=bv.71198958,d.aWw.

41. Organization for Economic Cooperation and Development (OECD) Global Forum on Competition, "Competition Issues in the Distribution of Pharmaceuticals," February 2014, http://www.oecd.org/competition/competition-distribution-pharmaceuticals.htm.

and adopt more sophisticated human resources benefits practices, health care and insurance is of increasing focus with businesses looking to provide insurance. This is driving demand for locally produced, more competitive, and cheaper drugs that can be sold domestically, and also for pharmaceuticals to sell internationally at U.S. Food and Drug Administration (FDA) standards.

The sector is still growing, and the market in Pakistan is almost evenly divided between national and multinational companies.[42] Despite some success of the pharmaceutical industry in Pakistan, there are several weaknesses and challenges. Of all the companies in the industry, about 100 of the top companies handle 90 percent of the business.[43] Research and development is severely lacking, and domestic patent law is significantly below international standards. This is where domestic pharmaceutical companies are looking for co-ventures with U.S. businesses. While U.S. businesses can provide expertise, Pakistani businesses can provide low costs and high margins. The government has been resistant to aligning domestic patent law with international standards, but given the increasing demand, it is likely that in the future the government will open this sector to more competition.

Local manufacturers are dependent on imported raw materials. This limits the sustainability and independence of the domestic market.[44] Pakistani businesses believe that U.S. investment could bring Pakistani raw materials up to par with FDA standards through training and creating bodies that will give FDA approval. The government highly regulates the industry, and has discouraged foreign investment by instilling a corporate income tax rate of 35 percent and a 15 percent tax on sales.[45] There is also strict government control over pricing.[46] However, trends indicate this is changing. For example, Pakistan typically grants special tariff and tax exemptions for pharmaceuticals that are not available domestically. Progressive patent expiration and implementation of trade agreements present promising growth opportunities for pharmaceutical manufacturers in the region. Many barriers to the flow of capital and international direct investment are gradually being removed. (See the Medipak Limited case study in Appendix B.)

---

42. Vaqar Ahmed, Samavia Batool, and Safwan Khan, "Pharmaceutical Trade with India," *India-Pakistan Trade Newsletter: Pharmaceutical Special*, 2013, http://www.sdpi.org/media/media_details1562-article-2013 .html.

43. Asma Khan and Masooz Subzwari, "Reverse Logistics in Pakistan's Pharmaceutical Sector," *South Asian Journal of Management Sciences* 3, no. 1 (Spring 2009): 27–36, http://iurc.edu.pk/sajms/issues/2009/Spring2009 V3N1P4.pdf.

44. Business Monitor International, *Pakistan: Pharmaceuticals and Healthcare Report* (London: Business Monitor International, 2010), http://www.google.com/url?sa=t&rct=j&q=&esrc=s&source=web&cd=7&ved=0CFEQ FjAG&url=http%3A%2F%2Fxa.yimg.com%2Fkq%2Fgroups%2F18751725%2F1377877507%2Fname%2Fpakistan &ei=723NU-ffFIaiyASnmoGwBg&usg=AFQjCNFrwKMMlraXkWuEwSMtN_fhiRzTxg&sig2=U786LctuPQ-dd1 XjcEVj2w&bvm=bv.71198958,d.aWw.

45. Ibid.

46. Business Wire, "Healthcare in Pakistan is Still in the Early Stages of Development with Widespread Poverty and a Weak Health System the Underlying Causes of the Poor Health Status of the Population," January 18, 2006, http://www.businesswire.com/news/home/20060118005406/en/Healthcare-Pakistan-Early-Stages -Development-Widespread-Poverty#.U82RYBbNUdI.

Real Estate

As Pakistan faces increasing urbanization, investments in real estate will only increase with time. The concept of high-rise apartment buildings is not particularly new, but the demand for such real estate is increasing quickly. Currently, 38 percent of the population lives in urban areas.[47] As urbanization occurs and consumer spending increases so too will the demand in the hospitality and retail sectors. There are already a number of foreign players in the real estate market for malls and apartment buildings, forcing competitive prices. Pakistan is one of only three countries in the Next Eleven that is increasing the push toward urbanization over the next 25 years.[48]

Renewable and Alternative Energy

There is a current shortage of 3,000 to 5,000 megawatts of electricity in Pakistan per year.[49] Power generation is sourced through a mix of thermal, hydroelectric (hydel), and nuclear power plants, with 49.9 percent of energy provided by natural gas, 31 percent oil, 7.6 percent coal, 10.6 percent hydro, 0.7 percent nuclear, and 0.1 percent renewable.[50]

The government of Pakistan has set a target to reach at least 5 percent of total commercial energy supplies through alternative and renewable energy by 2030.[51] The government has established a number of incentive structures to encourage investment in this sector. For example, the government provides indirect tax relief in which there is no custom duty or sales tax for plant infrastructure, machinery, equipment, and spares.[52] The power policy in Pakistan offers incentives of approximately 18 percent internal rate of return (IRR) on equity in certain renewable energy projects along with long-term offtake agreements—essentially, a promise that there will be a buyer once production starts—backed by sovereign guarantees from the government of Pakistan and in some cases even from the provincial governments.[53] Where a company establishes an industrial undertaking for installation of any plant machinery or equipment to be used to generate alternative energy, accelerated depreciation of 90 percent is allowed for the first operation. Additionally, there is a 100 percent income tax credit for newly established industrial undertakings for the first five

47. Government of Pakistan, Ministry of Finance, "Pakistan Economic Survey 2012–13," http://www .finance.gov.pk/survey_1213.html.

48. Sandra Lawson, Davide Heacock, and Anna Stupnytska, "Beyond the BRICS: A look at the 'Next 11,'" in *BRICS and Beyond*, ed. Jim O'Neill (New York: Goldman Sachs, 2007), 159–164, http://www.goldmansachs.com/our -thinking/archive/archive-pdfs/brics-book/brics-chap-13.pdf.

49. Bigger Picture Consulting, "Energy Sector Profile, 2014." Provided to author by CEO Adil Waqas.

50. Faiz M. Bhutta, "Renewable Energy Opportunities and Challenges in Pakistan," AltEnergyMag.com, October/November 2013, http://www.altenergymag.com/emagazine/2013/10/renewable-energy-opportunities -and-challenges-in-pakistan/2159.

51. Government of Pakistan, Ministry of Water and Power, "Alternative and Renewable Energy Policy, 2011," http://www.aedb.org/midtermpolicy.htm.

52. KPMG, "Pakistan—alternative energy incentives, tax compliance improvements," May 15, 2014, http://www.kpmg.com/global/en/issuesandinsights/articlespublications/mesa-tax-update/pages/pakistan -alternative-energy-incentives.aspx.

53. Bigger Picture Consulting, "Energy Sector Profile, 2014."

years of operations.[54] Challenges in this sector include a lack of adequate financing for renewable projects and corruption.[55]

The government of Pakistan is also promoting investments in wind power generation, coal, and hydel, with each having varying degrees of incentives for private investment. Across the sectors, the government of Pakistan is allowing a high rate of ownership and debt (80:20 debt to equity leverage); sovereign guarantees of returns on equity of 15 percent IRR on furnace oil–based projects, 17 percent IRR on coal-based projects, and 20 percent on wind energy projects.[56] Pakistan has tremendous potential for generating energy through wind projects. If developed, the Sindh wind corridor (the Gharo-Keti Bandar wind corridor) on its own can generate up to 40,000 megawatts per year of wind electricity.[57]

Because Pakistan also has the seventh largest reserves of coal in the world, the Pakistani government is trying to address the energy deficit through coal.[58] Coal is a politically contentious topic in the United States, so many U.S. entrepreneurs may not want to enter into any co-ventures or investments due to a potential backlash in the United States. One avenue to consider is transfers of technologies to make coal power more eco-friendly. Opportunities exist as well for solar energy, particularly in Southern Punjab and Baluchistan, which are some of the most underserved and dangerous places in Pakistan. U.S. investors may consider direct investments in these areas to be risky, so co-ventures would be preferable. While local partners can mitigate the risks, there are the added incentives of low recurring costs, lower initial capital outlays compared to hydel, and an already present demand.

A successful example of investing in the energy market is that of Abraaj Group and Karachi Electric Supply Company (KESC) in 2008 when Abraaj was hired to staunch the US$15 million per month outflows that KESC was facing. Abraaj restructured KESC, while improving its bottom line. Abraaj bought a 50 percent stake in KESC power and committed US$361million over three years. They "targeted capital expenditures to improve system efficiency and rationalized the tariff structure to improve cash flow management."[59] As a result, losses were reduced. Integrated business centers were developed to merge the commercial and technical sides of the business, and put in new management systems to improve performance and efficiency.[60]

---

54. KPMG, "Pakistan—alternative energy incentives, tax compliance improvements."
55. Bhutta, "Renewable Energy Opportunities and Challenges in Pakistan."
56. KPMG, *Investment in Pakistan.*
57. Alternative Energy Development Board, "Wind Energy in Pakistan," http://www.aedb.org/wind.htm.
58. Associated Press of Pakistan, "Pakistan ranked 7th in world having coal reserves," *Business Recorder*, November 13, 2013, http://www.brecorder.com/pakistan/business-a-economy/144400-pakistan-ranked-7th-in-world-having-coal-reserves.html.
59. Emerging Markets Private Equity Association (EMPEA), "Case Study: Karachi Electric Supply Company (Pakistan)," n.d., http://www.abraaj.com/images/uploads/newspdfs/EMPEA_case_study_kesc_web_FINAL.PDF.
60. Ibid.

The Mining Sector

GEMS

Pakistan is home to many semi-precious gemstones and some of the world's most valuable emeralds. While the gemstone trade is centuries old and part of the old Silk Route, today there remain some challenges, which are in fact opportunities for investment. Most of these challenges remain at the source. The methods used to mine gem stones remain archaic, with gem dealers paying not only for raw stone, but also for any waste created during the mining process. Individuals interviewed by the author pointed out that U.S. investment would yield mutual benefits in the following areas. First, technology transfers would improve mining efficiency. Second, technology transfers would improve craftsmanship. Third, technology could refine the cutting and shaping of gemstones. Opportunities might then exist as well for co-ventures at the higher end of the market, resulting in the sale of high-quality jewelry.

MARBLE

Much like gemstones, Pakistani businesses are looking for alternative ways to extract marble. The current practice of blasting is wasteful. There is an opening for U.S. investment in infrastructure, which would link the mines to the port cities. Currently, the opportunities lie in investing with businesses through technology transfers for more efficient mining and refinement.

Low-Cost Private Education

In recent years there has been a significant increase in the number of low-cost private schools (LCPSs) in developing countries, including Pakistan.[61] Nongovernment schools have proliferated in developing countries to meet excess demand resulting from an insufficient supply of public school spaces or to provide alternatives to a failing public education system.[62] Private education initiatives are often a response to local parental demand, and the popular perception in Pakistan is that quality is superior in private schools compared to government schools.[63] As the middle class has grown, a large segment of society does not feel adequately served by the education sector, and this segment can pay more than the average PKR (Pakistani Rupee) 1,200 per month charged by public schools.

All roundtable participants and many individuals interviewed pointed out the investment potential in low-cost private education (LCPE) in Pakistan. Profits in LCPE in general do not come from high tuition fees but from low costs and the large scale of Pakistan's

---

61. Aban Haq and Khadija Ali, "Financing Low-Cost Private Schools (LCPS) through Microfinance," Micro Note No. 21, Pakistan Microfinance Network, March 2014, http://www.microfinanceconnect.info/assets/articles/5b1cc9ff056a1ff794fd647aeb3b2280.pdf.

62. Stephen P. Heyneman and Jonathan M.B. Stern, "Low Cost Private Schools for the Poor: What public policy is appropriate?," *International Journal of Educational Development* 35 (2013): 3–15.

63. Institute of Social and Policy Sciences (I-SAPS), *Private Sector Education in Pakistan: Mapping and Musing* (Islamabad: I-SAPS, 2010), http://workspace.unpan.org/sites/internet/Documents/UNPAN92664.pdf.

demand and need for education with its current demographic structure. It is estimated that Pakistan has close to 5.1 million children out of school, while government spending on the sector has been limited to a mere 2.3 percent of gross national product (GNP) in 2011.[64]

The Pakistani government recognizes the urgency and need for education. For years it has allowed an "adopt a school" model. However, this model was predominantly based on philanthropic money and hence is not a tenable long-term solution. Now both the private sector and the government are looking for investments and co-ventures, not just for traditional education but also for specialized vocational training.

Despite growth and increasing interest in the LCPE model, there are several significant challenges. Some of the main constraints include lack of access to funding, shortage of skilled and qualified professions to teach, difficulty in accessing infrastructure and land, bureaucratic hurdles, and government regulations and policies.[65] Additionally, there is significant financial risk when investing in LCPE. Private schools that accommodate low-income students are at risk of financial failure because frequently they depend on tuition or private income from the original founder of the school.[66] Often this is an unsustainable model. Due to the risk, banks and other lending institutions are reluctant to engage in long-term planning or investment.[67] And on the medium-sized entrepreneur side, the costs of lending are very high, as noted before. An additional weakness in the LCPE model is the lack of regulation or education standards. Most LCPE schools in Pakistan are unregistered.[68] (For an example of an entrepreneur who has entered this market and navigated the challenges, see the American School of International Academics [ASIA] case study in Appendix B.)

Given the risks associated with LCPE in Pakistan, the best investments would be through co-ventures with existing schools or vocational training institutions. These investments or co-ventures could be through (1) curriculum sharing (particularly for schools to bring the students up to par with the best schools in Pakistan), (2) technology to improve the efficiency of educational services, or (3) direct investments into schools. The U.K. Department for International Development (DFID) conducted a study of LCPE and found that there was plenty of potential for investments or co-ventures. Recognizing the risks, the Pakistani government can also offer special returns on different types of educational investments. For example, the prevalent product features include loan tenures of 12 to 24 months, a grace period of three months to allow the school to acquire relevant equipment, skills, and staff with an effective interest rate of 27 percent.[69]

Organizations in the United States could use their power to leverage and create information repositories profitably for the education system. As mentioned in the introduction

---

64. Haq and Ali, "Financing Low-Cost Private Schools (LCPS) through Microfinance."
65. International Finance Corporation (IFC), *Education Investment Guide: A Guide for Investors in Private Education in Emerging Markets* (Washington, DC: IFC, 2010), http://www.ifc.org/wps/wcm/connect/ddd76080 4970bf219702d7336b93d75f/EduInvestGuide.pdf?MOD=AJPERES.
66. Heyneman and Stern, "Low Cost Private Schools for the Poor."
67. Ibid.
68. Haq and Ali, "Financing Low-Cost Private Schools (LCPS) through Microfinance."
69. Ibid.

(see Chapter 1), where there are gaps there are also opportunities. For example, many institutions find it hard to lend to low-cost private schools because of the lack of records and financial statements. Risks are hard to mitigate because they are often national level issues. Thus, the profitable solutions may actually be best executed in conjunction with the national and local governments and USAID (who have a history of successes in the education sector) and Pakistan's private and social sector.[70]

There are a number of issues that need to be addressed in financing private education:[71]

- *Developing a strategy for entering the market.* It is important to understand the structure and context of the national education system. The main players are the Pakistani private sector, the government, and donors such as USAID, DFID, and the World Bank that have done extensive mapping studies on Pakistan's educational needs.

- *Identifying the target market.* The best information for this will come from the private sector itself locally and where U.S. businesses or entrepreneurs feel that their investment or co-venture will have the strongest strategic advantage.

- *Raising workforce productivity by instituting appropriate processes and adopting a standardized solutions approach.* Where Pakistani entrepreneurs such as Ayesha Hamid and Seema Aziz can help map out the landscape, U.S. investments or co-ventures can be profitable in designing more efficient systems to manage defaults.

- *Identifying and targeting the strongest private schools and colleges as potential clients.* The best way to approach this is to let the Pakistani private sector do this, so that any investments or co-ventures are demand driven.

- *Developing a robust risk framework.* This is required to ensure that the quality of the portfolio is not compromised and sales targets are met without making dangerous loans. In this case, private sector to private sector engagement will be most valuable. Pakistani entrepreneurs have the risk exposure and the know-how to mitigate political and community risk. On the U.S. side, policies, processes, and technologies that ensure quality and efficiency will be profitable and valuable.

The Retail Sector

Despite the global economic downturn in 2008 and Pakistan's weak economy, the retail sector in Pakistan was growing at about 7 percent per year even in 2012.[72] With a number of mid- to high-end retail franchises opening and experiencing rapid growth in recent

---

70. See the case study of Ayesha Hamid's American School of International Academics (ASIA) in Appendix B.
71. All issues have been identified from IFC, *Education Investment Guide.*
72. Shamira Shackle, "Banking on History, British Brands Thrive in Pakistan," *Dawn,* December 5, 2012, http://www.dawn.com/news/769067/banking-on-history-british-brands-thrive-in-pakistan.

years, there are expectations that the higher end of the retail sector will continue to grow, with mid-end clothing retailers doing especially well. Many individuals interviewed for this report agreed that Pakistan can become a stable market for high-end luxury goods such as watches and designer handbags as investments in the retail sector increase.[73]

---

73. See case study on Dynasty Ltd. in Appendix B.

3 | Conclusion

As mentioned in the introduction (see Chapter 1), engaging with the private sector in Pakistan is beneficial to a number of stakeholders. This report focused on the investment perspective (and less so on the trade perspective). This report is of course for general consumption but particularly targets investors, chambers of commerce and industry, USAID and its private-sector development programs, and government bodies related to investment such as the Overseas Private Investment Corporation (OPIC) in the United States and the board of investment of the Pakistani government. This report should not be treated as a guide to investing but is instead a study that focuses on the potential in Pakistan and the competitive sectors, and research that will begin increased policy dialogue of connecting medium sized entrepreneurs on both sides.

There are two reasons why the focus is on medium-sized entrepreneurs. First, mid-sized Pakistani entrepreneurs have at least some track record of success. They are more likely to have documentation, are able to absorb investment, and have already navigated the investment and regulatory environment in Pakistan. Second, medium-sized entrepreneurs in the United States do not necessarily have the risk exposure or the ability to take on unknown political and community risks, which is why medium-sized entrepreneurs in Pakistan with their expertise can help. Generally for both sides, as the BRICS countries heat up and face increasing inflation and costs, the flow of capital toward frontier markets has already increased, particularly for the Next Eleven, which includes Pakistan.

There is immense scope for collaboration using existing, yet underutilized, tools. For example, the trade and commerce departments of the embassies in both countries could gather more information and more aggressively disseminate this information to the relevant stakeholders such as the chambers of commerce and industry in both countries. Another repository of information that is underutilized are the feasibility studies undertaken by USAID for private-sector development programs. These should be made easily available to investors and concerned stakeholders. Interagency flows of information could be immensely productive. The U.S. Trade and Development Authority (USTDA) conducts feasibility studies for small and medium enterprises (SMEs). These could be enhanced further by taking into account OPIC's strategy and USAID priorities.

More generally for frontier markets that are strategically important, like Pakistan, OPIC should have a first loss equity fund particularly related to the sectors that OPIC itself has invested in. This shows two things. First, it sends a positive signal to U.S. entrepreneurs that the sectors are viable and increases investor confidence. Second, it provides additional risk mitigation for entrepreneurs, a service that would be appreciated by medium-sized entrepreneurs who are developing their expertise in frontier markets. At this time only the Development Credit Authority can give partial risk guarantees and some assistance in first loss equity funding. Pakistan, like many other countries, has been a recipients of "enterprise funds" via USAID that are public-private partnerships to support entrepreneurship. These funds have typically not fared well. Medium-sized enterprises might be better served under OPIC, rather than USAID, because it deals more directly with the private sector.[1]

However, the Pakistan Private Investment Initiative (PPII), with its more innovative approach of promoting self-sustaining private equity deals, is a step in the right direction. It is still too soon to gauge whether this program has been successful but more programs that engage the private sector to assist other private-sector actors should be explored. From a security perspective, continued and increased economic activity will serve two purposes. First, if the well-being of the burgeoning Pakistani entrepreneurs is tied to the well-being and economic health of the United States, Pakistanis will be more vested in keeping U.S. interests in mind. Second, as the emerging economies become more powerful, the United States will have to engage more with Next Eleven countries, which includes Pakistan.

Beyond security and nuclear weapons, Pakistan and the United States both share similar goals—to benefit each other's economies. This report is, hopefully, a step toward exploring new, exciting, and profitable ventures.

---

1. Author interview with senior USAID official, April 2014. Also see Benjamin Leo, Todd Moss, and Beth Schwanke, "OPIC Unleashed: Strengthening US Tools to Promote Private-Sector Development Overseas," Center for Global Development, August 2013, http://www.cgdev.org/sites/default/files/OPIC-Unleashed-final.pdf.

Appendix A: Economic Facts and Figures

Table A.1. Foreign Direct Investment (FDI) Inflows in Pakistan from United States by Economic Group, July 2011–May 2012

Sector	FDI (US$ million)
Construction	28.5
Beverages	28.4
Communications	21.0
Chemicals	20.3
Trade	19.7
Financial Business	13.6
Oil and Gas Exploration	12.7
Personal Services	9.9
Food	8.6
Electronics	5.9
Textiles	5.7
Others	34.9
Total	209.2

Source: Pakistan Board of Investment (BOI), http://boi.gov.pk.

Table A.2. Percent of Total Employment of Pakistan's Labor Force

Sector	2006–2007	2007–2008	2008–2009	2009–2010	2010–2011	2011–2012
Agriculture	43.61	44.65	45.1	45.0	45.1	43.7
Manufacturing	13.54	12.99	13.0	13.2	13.7	14.1
Construction	6.56	6.29	6.6	6.7	7.0	7.4
Wholesale/retail			16.5	16.3	16.2	14.4
Transport, storage, communication		5.39	5.46	5.1	5.2	5.5
Social services	14.41	13.66	11.2	11.2	10.8	13.3
Other	2.06	0.10	2.4	2.4	2.1	1.6

Source: Government of Pakistan, Ministry of Finance, "Pakistan Economic Survey 2012–13," http://finance.gov.pk/survey/chapters_13/12-Population.pdf.

Table A.3. U.S. Direct Investment Abroad (US$ million)

Country	2004	2005	2006	2007	2008	2009	2010	2011	2012
All Countries	2,160,844	2,241,656	2,477,268	2,993,980	3,232,493	3,565,020	3,741,910	4,084,659	4,453,307
Nigeria	1,936	1,105	1,677	1,584	3,254	4,938	5,058	5,307	8,152
Libya	58	247	1,664	1,676	(D)	(D)	2,719	1,964	2,315
Lebanon	156	169	151	179	214	150	203	206	173
Afghanistan	6	6	6	6	6	3	3	3	3
Pakistan	858	1,130	1,167	(D)	430	624	(D)	254	218
Bangladesh	354	181	365	218	260	331	296	(D)	368

(D) = data not available.

Source: Information collected from U.S. department of Commerce, Bureau of Economic Analysis, http://www.bea.gov/international/di1usdbal.htm.

Table A.4. Overseas Private Investment Corporation (OPIC) Investments in Pakistan, 2004–2014

Year	Project Name	Sector	Investment (US$)
2012	Aga Khan Hospital & Medical College Fund	Finance	30,000,000
2012	Pakistan Mobile Communications Limited	Finance	30,000,000
2012	SSLD BioEnergy	Finance	16,700,000
2011	Tameer Microfinance Bank Limited	Finance	21,500,000
2011	TPL Properties (Pvt.) Limited	Finance	20,000,000
2010	Chemonics International	Insurance	3,125,000
2010	Hyperbaric Technologies, Inc	Insurance	21,600
2010	Towershare (Pvt.) Limited	Finance	9,792,000
2009	none		
2008	Tameer Microfinance Bank Limited	Finance	5,000,000
2008	Directorate General Procurement	Insurance	27,630
2007	American International School System	Insurance	3,500,000
2007	The Asia Foundation	Insurance	144,947
2007	Tameer Mirco Finance Bank Limited	Finance	10,000,000
2007	Pakistan Water and Power	Insurance	29,820,000
2007	American International School System	Finance	2,500,000
2007	Kashf Foundation	Finance	4,999,500
2007	Engro Vopak Terminal Ltd.	Finance	16,500,000
2007	Relief International Branch Office	Insurance	139,014
2006	none		
2005	Pakistan Mortgage Guaranty Trust	Finance	3,750,000
2005	Emerging Markets Consulting (Private) Limited	Finance	6,500,000
2005	Sweetwater Pakistan (Private) Limited	Finance	3,000,000
2004	Sweetwater Pakistan (Private) Limited	Insurance	1,125,900
2004	International Rescue Committee, Inc.	Insurance	807,482

Source: Current OPIC projects by year, http://www.opic.gov/opic-action/current-opic-projects.

Appendix B. Case Studies

Financial Services

CASE STUDY: AKD SECURITIES LTD.

AKD Securities Ltd. was the first brokerage house to launch an online trading platform in Pakistan. It has the largest market share of approximately 6,000 customers and almost 6 percent of the daily average of trading in value terms. AKD Securities provides equity brokerage, economic and securities research, and investment banking and financial advisory services.[1]

Farid Alam, Chief Executive Officer (CEO), AKD Securities Ltd.

How and why did you join this company in 2007? What is your professional background?

I am a chartered accountant with over two decades of firsthand experience in financial markets. I was lured into this profession by my love of auditing. I aced my B.Com examinations at Punjab University. I started out as a CFO [chief financial officer], then moved to corporate finance, and then ultimately to the equity department as equity strategist. For this position I moved to Karachi, which is the financial hub of the country.

What were the challenges and what were the opportunities? How did you capitalize on the opportunities and overcome the challenges?

The capital market in Pakistan is sometimes mistakenly thought to represent only the equities market. Some of the other important and larger portions of the capital markets, such as the debt market, have not been able to either grow or, for that matter, glow. This is a great challenge for professionals like me and for organizations like ours: to rise to the occasion and introduce products beyond the plain vanilla cash-based equity products. This revision in our strategy is likely to increase participation by retail investors, thereby increasing the length and breadth of the capital markets.

---

1. For more information, see AKD Securities Ltd., "About us," http://www.akdsecurities.net/overview.aspx.

What could you not capitalize on? And has this changed?

Corporatization is a big challenge in companies, which are often family run. In the "post-2008 financial tsunami," family businesses have come to accept that it is less painful for them to lose money, if it happens as a result of their own decisions, compared to facing the same fate at the hands of professional management. This seems more like a psychological rather than a professionally explainable management phenomenon.

Please share your key business strategies that have led you to this current stature.

I believe that for any organization looking for success, it is imperative for its leader to take charge of the direction leading to the achievement of the long-term goals. We developed an in-house ability to plan beyond the present, converting our entire team into becoming passionate about one objective: that of making our company infallible under all odds. This created a synergy among us, which even under the most testing times, particularly between 2008 and 2011, led us to sit down together and asses the needs of the changing dynamics of equity markets, evaluate the appetite of retail investors, and align resources and efforts toward providing the best possible IT solution to our online retail division AKD-Trade. Today, we have thousands of active and immensely satisfied retail customers of AKD-Trade, apart from our prestigious foreign and local institutional and high net worth individuals. Over the years, this strategy has paid off, translating the results into generating for us significantly higher volumes of business, culminating into appreciable increased brokerage revenues. Based on this experience, I can safely declare that success emanates from competitive leadership.

How did you connect with foreign partners?

At present, AKD Securities provides a full suite of services including investment banking, research, and equity brokering to clients ranging from domestic retail investors, high net worth individuals, and foreign institutional funds. The latter are largely tapped through a network of partner broker/dealers (governed under chaperoning agreements) while some service offerings to foreign investors include conference calls with corporate managements, organizing investor conferences, and periodic roadshows to major global financial centers. This has enabled AKD Securities to emerge with an increasing market share in international business.

Do you have the high performance team with the right skill set, mind-set, and value set to lead the business growth?

The growth of our company and thousands of our satisfied customers leads us to believe that we have just the right people doing the right job, at the right time. We have a young and dynamic team of professionals in place, who have the passion to succeed and lead from the front. Our team has to its credit several innovative capital market transactions, along with top of the line brokerage and investment research services.

Have your efforts been recognized and acknowledged?

Yes, our efforts have not gone unnoticed. We have received accolades from a number of prestigious professional institutions and associations such as the CFA Association of Pakistan, the Institute of Chartered Accountants of Pakistan (ICAP) and the *Asia Money* magazine. Last year, we were ranked as the "Best Corporate Finance House of the Year" and "Runners-up Best Brokerage House of the Year" by the CFA Association. This year, we were awarded the "Best Transaction of the Year" title by the ICAP, at the ICAP Excellence Awards 2013, for being the financial advisor and arranger for the issuance of participation term certificates by Treet Corporation Limited.

How did you grow? What are you products now? How are you planning on expanding/ diversifying your products?

Over the last decade or so, we have expanded into a full-service corporate brokerage house with growth impetus now being provided by investment banking mandates, online retail brokering and international sales. Specifically, our online trading platform was launched in 2002 and today is one of the market leaders in this space. There is still immense potential in this area where the number of domestic retail investors remains paltry compared to the number of bank accounts (less than 40 million) and much lower compared to the number of cellular subscribers (130 million). This will remain a focus area going forward where AKD Securities has and will continue to take part in local investor awareness programs. At the same time, we intend to keep our aggressive stance on increasing market share in the international business where we are looking to leverage existing broker dealer partnerships and our quality research. Outside of commercial banks, AKD Securities Ltd. is one of the biggest capital market firms in the country. AKD Securities is the leader in raising and providing risk capital in underwriting, market making, and mergers and acquisitions in Pakistan. In this regard, since 2009, AKD Securities has been the market leader in IPOs (Initial Public Offering) where focus will continue to remain on introducing quality names to the local bourses.

Where do you see the market going? What opportunities are there for collaboration with large and medium entrepreneurs in the United States?

The local stock markets have been in an extended bull run since the lows of early 2009 and investors have enjoyed magnificent returns. Over the last five years, the KSE 100 Index has delivered a 32 percent return CAGR. (Compound Annual Growth Rate). During this same time, brokers have done well, but average daily traded volumes are still almost half as much as those in the heady days of 2005 to 2007. There is still an opportunity on this front where the regulator can look to address this issue so that brokerage houses are able to reflect the ongoing bull run at the markets. In terms of collaborations with U.S. entrepreneurs, space for broker dealer partnerships exists.

Generally in the economy, where are the opportunities for growth and international investment?

We believe there is immense growth potential in the economy if the government of Pakistan focuses on big-ticket infrastructure development projects and if the private-sector credit offtake cycle revives. We are positive that these changes will materialize where we believe cyclical sectors such as construction, auto, and commercial banks are headed for an uplift over the medium-term. These areas could witness increased international investment (particularly FPI [foreign private investment]) while traditional FDI [foreign direct investment] focus on the oil and gas sector should remain. In addition, the textile space appears to be registering on the radars of Chinese investors and this could morph into a trend if other players also start taking an interest in the sector particularly after the approval of the EU's GSP Plus Scheme.

What was your experience with private equity (PE) and venture capital (VC)? Do you think going forward there is potential for VC and PE in Pakistan?

PE/VC have not taken off properly in Pakistan, which can be contributed to a low level of financial sophistication and cultural disinclination toward entrepreneurship. That said, this remains an exciting field where VC/PE firms definitely have a future in Pakistan if they take a long-term view and also provide advice on running the businesses. Areas that appear particularly ripe for such ventures include corporate farming, education, and health care.

CASE STUDY: SAFEWAY FUND LTD.

Safeway Fund Ltd. is an asset management company that provides management services for two funds: Asian Stocks Fund and Safeway Mutual Fund. In 2013, Reuters ranked both funds among the top 25 performing equity funds in the world in 2012.[2]

Nihal Cassim, CEO, Safeway Fund Ltd., interview

How and why did you enter your market in 2010?

I joined Safeway Fund Ltd. as CEO in August 2008, in the wake of the stock market crisis. Safeway Fund Ltd. is an asset management company based in Karachi, Pakistan. We manage two open-end equity mutual funds—Asian Stocks Fund (ASF) and Safeway Mutual Fund (SMF), which have a combined portfolio size of US$15 million. We were quick in taking measures to shield ourselves from the growing crisis and by early 2010 with success: I bought the company from the existing sponsors. Being third generation of a family that has been central to Pakistan's equity markets, I have a lot of experience with equity

---

2. For more information, see Safeway Fund Ltd., "Welcome to Safeway Fund Limited," www.safewayfund.com.

market investments and advisory and corporate transactions. That is why I bought the company when the opportunity arose.

What were the challenges and what were the opportunities? How did you capitalize on the opportunities and overcome the challenges? What could you not capitalize on? And has this changed?

The biggest challenge in 2008–2009 was survival. As a first-time CEO, I had to make decisions about cost cutting and downsizing. It was a very difficult time and I concluded that better coherence between the business, its shareholders, and the employees was necessary. It was important to retain the good members of the team and to give the shareholders a fair return.

We undertook aggressive cost cuts, guaranteed the shareholders a certain return, paid aggressive bonuses to top performers, streamlined our policies, and trimmed our balance sheet to be more effective and dynamic. We also took stock of the equity markets and made aggressive investments in our own equity mutual funds by levering up our balance sheet. With time, as the equity markets rebounded, our fee income and investments in the funds grew rapidly.

We would have liked to have grown further through merger or acquisition of weaker industry participants; however regulatory policy is not conducive to such aggressiveness, as yet, but this is set to change due to market pressures.

Rankings/Accomplishments?

As shown in the table below, the funds under management of the company have performed exceptionally well.

	2014*	2013	2012	2011	2010
Total funds in Pakistan	154	140	140	133	120
Safeway performance ranking	4	4	4	45	6
Safeway return	40.8%	63.2%	28.0%	13.0%	28.0%
Asian performance ranking	5	5	6	41	5
Asian return	37.5%	63.1%	27.5%	14.7%	29.1%

*Nine months.[3]
Source: JSIL Research Performance Table and SFL Calculations.

In 2013, Reuters ranked both funds among the top 25 performing equity funds in the world in 2012.

---

3. At the time that this case study was written, only nine months of the fiscal year had passed.

Where do you see the market going? What opportunities are there for collaboration with large and medium entrepreneurs in the United States? Generally in the economy, where are the opportunities for growth and international investment? Are there legal and administrative barriers that can easily be overcome?

We are bullish on the Pakistan economy. We believe that the government is taking the right steps in phasing out energy subsidies, as these have led to inefficient use of resources. Once eliminated, the bottlenecks in the energy chain will be identifiable. Besides corruption and security, energy subsidies and shortages have been the primary things affecting Pakistan's economic growth. It is also worth noting that Pakistan's high inflation over the past few years arose largely because of increases in international commodity prices and by gradual, non-recurring costs of increasing prices through subsidy removal. As these gradual, non-recurring elements are getting absorbed, inflation is falling. With regards to decreasing corruption, sentiment is that there would be less of it within the current administration. With regards to security, no meaningful plan has been put forth, the uncertainty of which creates opportunities.

In terms of investment opportunities (outside of equity markets) for U.S.-based entrepreneurs, we see the following opportunities for smart money investors:

- Construction and ancillary sectors. This includes housing development for low and middle income families. At present Pakistan has an approximate shortage of 1 million homes. Opportunities also exist in supplying prefabricated materials to speed up the pace of construction.

- Logistical and storage services for the transport of food products from the ports in the south to upcountry (and vice versa). This could be further specialized into cold storage chains, warehousing outside major metropolis for further distribution into the metropolis, warehousing in collaboration with banks, and issuing warehousing receipts, etc.

- Buying into government long term debt. Current yields are 7 percent in U.S. dollar terms for the Eurobond and 12 to 13 percent in rupee terms for PIBs (Pakistan investment bonds). Returns could be enhanced by lower expected inflation and an aggressive attempt by the government to break the culture of hoarding U.S. money.

- Opportunities to participate in the government's privatization program through buy out of select businesses.

- Playing into Pakistan's growing demographics through building schools, hospitals, and 2,000 square feet supermarkets with longer shopping hours.

I believe that the legal and administrative costs of investing in the identified sectors are quite low. In addition, I would suggest investing with someone who has demonstrated integrity and a good business sense.

CASE STUDY: I.Q. VENTURES

I.Q. Ventures is essentially a venture capital firm that also provides other services such as running a livestock company called I.Q. Green Farms, a platform for financial trading (I.Q. Capital). and an agri-fuel and energy commodities trading platform (I.Q. Trading).

Salman Haider Sheikh, CEO, I.Q. Ventures

How did you start in your field of work?

After working on Wall Street for 10 years at large investment banks like Merrill Lynch, Janney, Montgomery & Scott, and Wachovia Bank, I moved to Pakistan for personal reasons in 2005. I worked as the CEO of Faysal Bank's asset management company from 2006 till 2012, which was ranked the 13th fastest growing company in Pakistan by All World Network. Our company Faysal Asset Management still did well due to personal investor care and prudent risk management and liquidity management. My experience from the 1997 crisis on Wall Street, and then the 2001 NASDAQ crisis, helped me forecast the liquidity crunch in the Pakistani financial markets. We remained the most liquid investment house in the country and won several awards.

How have you grown? Can you give examples of partnerships?

In 2012, I moved to Islamabad from Karachi and decided to start a venture capital fund called I.Q. Ventures. My idea was to incubate new ideas within a controlled environment and ensure sustainable growth, strong corporate governance, and innovation. So far we have launched a livestock company under I.Q. Green Farms, a platform for financial trading under I.Q. Capital and an agri-fuel and energy commodities trading platform under I.Q. Trading. We have partnered with providing investment consulting to a private equity firm, Emkaan Investments (Saudi family fund) in Dubai. This partnership, along with other partnerships with similar PE platforms in the region, will ensure exit for our ventures by PE firms or M&A activity in the medium to long term. We are now contemplating I.Q. Foods to enter the restaurant and food export business as well.

The opportunities were highlighted by the professionals working in the respective fields whether livestock business lacking professional breeding techniques for goat-rearing and addressing the billion-dollar day in Pakistan on Eid when over $1 billion worth of animals are sacrificed on one day. We couldn't find any other industry with a consistent billion-dollar day in any other industry and decided that it was a huge opportunity. The other opportunity was lack of corporate farms for goats. The country had invested in milk and poultry production, but goat farming still remained a fragmented business.

On the commodities trading platform we have realized that shortage of gas supply and lack of further exploration along with rising cost of fuel has given rise to alternate fuels for our industrial base. We are involved in cross-provincial trade of agriculture waste as fuel for the boilers of industries in Punjab. The agriculture waste is procured in Sindh and supplied to Punjab. Now we are looking to diversify with coal and are looking to modernize and revolutionize the business with import of rice husk briquette machines from China and setting up small units in Sindh.

Where do you see the market going? What opportunities are there for collaboration with large and medium entrepreneurs in the United States?

I see the market moving toward India, China, Pakistan, and Bangladesh. Soon half of the world['s population] will be living in this region. Growth is eminent. Basic necessities for local consumption are going to increase exponentially. Production for the rest of the world with cheaper labor costs will remain in place with a rising population. Opportunities for investment are in every sector because modernization and streamlined structures are required in most of the fields. The fastest opportunities are in the field of technology because it is easier to transfer technologies which require less cost, such as mobile phones.

Any investor looking to do business in Pakistan must look for strong and structured local partners with a strong management team and some type of management control on ground. It is essential to do business face-to-face in Eastern countries. Due to the lack of regulatory framework or judicial framework, and the implementation and enforcement of contracts, international investors must ensure strong management of the ventures they invest in. It is the management that makes a business stand out as ideas can easily be replicated and competition with low barriers to entry is eminent.

The Pakistani government should initiate further co-study and real exchange programs of innovative entrepreneurs to encourage Pakistani entrepreneurs learning from U.S. entrepreneurs' experiences. This can be done by visits to [the United States] and Pakistan between entrepreneurs but this should focus on learning the processes of development. [The] U.S. government and business can initiate further programs profitably and assist [the] Pakistani regulatory environment to ensure that we have an institutional "venture capital" funds in Pakistan investing in new ideas and companies. More than 60 percent of young population in Pakistan cannot be provided jobs by the government or the current private sector and entrepreneurial and small business ideas are the only way to ensure economic viability of this growing population eradicating further lawlessness and issues like poverty alleviation.

Logistics

CASE STUDY: TCS PVT. LTD. [4]

TCS Pvt. Ltd. is a logistics company with offices in Pakistan, Canada, the United Arab Emirates (UAE), and the United Kingdom. TCS provides a number of services: domestic express services for overnight deliveries; worldwide express services; supply chain solutions through warehouse and distribution services; Sentiments, which caters for specific packages for holidays, gifts, and other celebrations with special rates; print and mail, also called MMS (mail management solutions), which is Pakistan's fastest digital bulk printing service; overland express for 40- and 50-foot containers; and Connect, which is an e-market place somewhat similar to Amazon.[5]

When and why was TCS started?

TCS was established by two brothers (Khalid Awan, a former pilot, and Sadiq Awan) in 1983 with headquarters in Karachi. It has since grown exponentially and began operation in the UAE in 1996 and Canada in 1999. TCS has four main products: domestic courier services, international courier services, overland shipping, and gift delivery. There were two reasons for the design of the TCS business model: first, to leverage IT services for supply chain management solutions to companies with assembly operations in Pakistan; and second, to act as an intermediary to link the fragmented but numerous small exporters to markets in North America and Europe.

How has TCS leveraged partnerships and co-ventures for its business?

TCS's first co-venture was with DHL. TCS took over operational control of DHL activities in Pakistan in the 1980s. Soon DHL Pakistan outperformed other DHL ventures in the region. Similarly, through partnerships with FedEx and DHL Far East, TCS provides a one-stop shop for a customer's entire courier needs. TCS is able to offer competitive prices because of its scale and ability to negotiate competitive prices with its partners. Also, to have a more uniform pricing structure (given that the courier rates differed across countries and were dependent on the competitive situation), TCS now couriers all its packages to its office in Dubai. They are then shipped internationally from Dubai. Today, TCS caters to almost every country in the world.

How has TCS leveraged a competitive and innovative financing model?

For the asset acquisition, TCS uses a leasing model due to existing tax benefits that accrue from leasing versus buying. Under Pakistani law, rent paid on leased assets is tax

---

4. All information for this case study comes from secondary research or the roundtables held. Secondary research is from Walter Kuemmerle and Zahid Ahmed, "TCS: An Entrepreneurial Air-Express Company in Pakistan," Case Study, Harvard Business School, April 22, 2004, http://www.tcscouriers.com/pk/CaseStudies/Default.aspx?qlink=9 ; and Nasir, "100 business leaders, entrepreneurs and difference makers of Pakistan."

5. For more information on what TCS does and its services, see www.tcscouriers.com.

deductible. This reduced the need for consistent large credit lines, given how capital intensive the logistics market is. To comply with State Bank of Pakistan (SBP) regulations, TCS uses a number of leasing companies, which also ensure competitiveness in the leasing pricing offered to TCS.

How does TCS ensure productivity, quality, and monitoring of its services?

TCS strives to be an outstanding service provider on par with the best logistics providers in the world such as FedEx, DHL, and UPS. It has a clear set of rules that state the corporate values. TCS has put in place a number of extremely innovative mechanisms and procedures to monitor productivity and quality. For logistics companies such as TCS, timely information sharing is critical. TCS has nearly 2,500 employees and communicates critical information along with paychecks to increase the likelihood of employees reading the information. Pakistan is a large country and also challenging at times, particularly for an information-based businesses. Because of the massive and diverse network of vendors catering to TCS, it also puts into place a self-employment scheme to ensure more effective monitoring for managers to track productivity at the individual level.

CASE STUDY: E2E SOLUTIONS

e2e Solutions is a supply chain management company that helps companies connect with other companies for maximum profit in all parts of the supply chain. Abid Butt founded e2e in February 2006 to tap what he foresaw was a "growing global market for movement of goods." His international expertise helped e2e grow its top line by a massive 1,918 percent between 2008 and 2010. In 2012, e2e achieved the title of becoming the fastest growing company in Pakistan by Harvard-based AllWorld Network. In just seven years it flourished as a group and earned the respect of businesses as the only "supply chain" conglomerate of Pakistan.

Abid Butt, founder and CEO, e2e Solutions, interview

How and why did you start your business in 2006? What was your core product?

The concept of e2e started in 2003 when I started thinking about giving end-to-end supply chain services to corporate entities in Pakistan—a market that was not being serviced at all at that time. The idea was to participate in the maximum part of customers' supply chains to give maximum bottom line positive impact and bring savings (both dollar and rupee savings) to them by acting in all parts of their supply chain. In February 2006, I partnered with a friend and started e2e Supply Chain Management from a one-room office in Karachi with only Rs 2 million as capital. Now, eight years later we have over 800 people and had a turnover of around $75 million in 2012. We have expanded into other countries like Afghanistan and Bangladesh and soon will have [a] presence in the UAE, India, Sri Lanka, and the Central Asian countries.

Today, Pakistan lags behind other countries in know-how and investment in the area of logistics. Given its strategic location, logistics is an important economic sector with significant growth and investment potential in Pakistan. It is also a key driver for private-sector development, economic growth, and overall development of the country. Indeed, one of the ways in which the state earns the confidence of the citizens is through effective logistics for service delivery. The gross domestic product (GDP) in Pakistan was 231 billion U.S. dollars in 2012, where services are the biggest sector of the economy and account for 53 percent of total GDP. According to a Data Monitor Report published in January 2011 Pakistan's logistics market is valued at $13 billion per annum.

We have also diversified into other businesses, "Agrimundi," which is a company involved in corporate farming and it derives value from increasing yield from modern farming techniques and by reducing the waste from farm to market (estimated to be 40 percent by the World Bank); Prime HRS, this is an HR [human resources] company focusing on recruitment, training, outsourcing, and consulting; e2e Business Enterprises is a company that will put up Pakistan's first Rice Bran (edible) Oil plant, utilizing rice bran which is wasted at the moment. In September 2013 we launched Pakistan Terminal Operators (PTO). This facility is the only dedicated tank cleaning and service depot in Pakistan.

Given Pakistan's strategic location, logistics is an important economic sector with significant growth and investment potential in Pakistan. The ISO[6] tank is one of the widely used tank containers by chemical, sugar, and oil industries for the transportation of hazardous and non-hazardous liquid cargo. In order to meet the myriad of complex deliveries required in these industries there lays a great opportunity for logistics companies in Pakistan to invest in the transportation and handling of the toxic and hazardous cargo.

In Pakistan these tanks were used in a single trip as there was an absence of a proper/professional cleaning/washing facility. [These tanks] require a specialized cleaning technology to clear out all odors and contamination in order to be reused for transportation.

e2e and Freight Connection Pvt. Ltd.[7] seized this business opportunity to offer a professionally run facility dedicated to cleaning, storage, repairs, and support services for ISO tanks. Founded in September 2013, Pakistan Terminal Operators (PTO) is the first ever and only certified cleaning station in Pakistan which has changed the dynamics of the liquid transportation industry. The tank station is designed to meet the standards for world-class performance and is equipped with the most modern techniques to minimize the environmental impact. The machinery for the cleaning station has been imported from the German company Weidner, internationally renowned for its pressure cleaning systems.

---

6. ISO is a standard for quality of tanks that use chemical and hazardous materials.
7. For more information on Freight Connection Pvt. Ltd., see www.fcppl.com.

What were the challenges and what were the opportunities? How did you capitalize on the opportunities and overcome the challenges?

Pakistan, like any other frontier market, brings its own set of challenges such as security, corruption (corporate and government), and poor implementation of the laws (contract enforceability)—but at the same time it's one of the most rewarding business environments. Sometimes being an entrepreneur in Pakistan feels like being a kid in a candy store—you want everything!

There are several issues as far as transport or trucking is concerned. First, there is a lack of policies and incentives to formalize the trucking industry and develop a modern warehousing infrastructure. Second, overloading and obsolete trucking fleets also continues to be a serious issue resulting in huge environmental and economic costs. Third, there is no structural program to provide funding for physical and technological infrastructure for warehousing, freight forwarding, and trucking sector. And fourth, logistics companies have to compete with the unregistered trucking companies.

How did you connect with foreign partners?

Internationally, our partners are Geodis Wilson. We have many small companies with which we partner in countries where Geodis does not operate. We connect with our foreign partners through:

- CEOs' international experience

- Other senior management international experience

- Traveling, knocking door-to-door

- References

Locally, our main partner is the Dawood Group in e2e Business and Enterprise. We have many other local partners. For one project we have partnered with Freight Connection of Rais Hasan Saadi Group of Dubai. Then in Agri Mundi our partners are the IT companies including Inbox, Creative Chaos, and Arpatech.

In December 2013, Geodis Wilson's regional vice president, Asia Pacific, Mathieu Renard Biron, visited Pakistan and held a range of bilateral discussions on the development of trade and logistics infrastructure in Pakistan with Punjab Chief Minister Shahbaz Sharif and Secretary Transport Punjab. Biron also explored business opportunities with one of the most prominent business leaders and philanthropist in Pakistan, Hussain Dawood, among many other business leaders.

Chief Minister Punjab showed interest in coal transportation as the current government has decided to convert power plants to coal and build new coal-based power plants.

In this regard, e2e is working on a paper to present to the Punjab government. The cost of coal transportation through trucks is very high. On the other hand, if rail transport is used it will be very cost effective. In Pakistan, railways carrying cargo account for less than 3 to 4 percent, whereas the average around the world is 25 percent.

The presence of a French logistics company can benefit the country on many fronts, including transfer of technology, improving transportation system, cold storage chains, storage, and warehousing. As preferred agent in Pakistan, e2e will enable its clients to fulfill their global reach and gain access to world-class transportation solutions, distribution and freight cost analysis, logistics management, and mission critical retail services.

The preferred agent status will definitely benefit our clients in opening new doors for them in the European and Asian market and access to cost-efficient rates in major shipping lines and airlines to any destination in the world. In return, e2e will provide Geodis Wilson with local market expertise and experience and a professional local sales force. For Geodis, the association with e2e will give them access to local knowledge, experience and expertise on Pakistan's logistics sector including information regarding trade policies [and] freight movements, [and] access to Pakistan's export and import data.

How did you grow? What are you products now? How are you planning on expanding/diversifying your products?

The first to introduce an array of visionary products and services, those that work with us, choose to embrace tomorrow with open arms; because one trendsetter recognizes another. Today, e2e is one of Pakistan's leading providers of end-to-end logistics services—literally from the shipper's door to the retailers' premises; specializing in international and local air-ocean freight. e2e's basic product range includes services in all areas of transport and logistics: international freight management, road transportation and warehousing, Afghan transit trade, supply chain management solutions.

In terms of business expansion the next step could be going into distribution. There might be a possibility for us to go into areas like commodity trading and public transport. We have already mentioned global expansion: Dubai, Central Asia, South Asia, and East Africa. These are the destinations we will be focusing [on] in the next three to four years depending on our financial capability. The expansion plan applies to our HR company, the logistics company, and the parent company. In addition, we have to consolidate our position in Pakistan to be number one. We want to get involved in other businesses by encouraging entrepreneurship.

CASE STUDY: ALTERNATE SOLUTIONS

Kashif Khan, CEO, Alternate Solutions

How and why did you start your business? What was your core product?

Alternate Solutions main focus is providing complete CSR [customer service representative] solutions to its clients and promoting entrepreneurship at all levels in collaboration with all relevant stakeholders. Alternate Solutions is also the partner organization that promotes Kauffman Foundation's biggest initiative, i.e., Global Entrepreneurship Week (GEW) in Pakistan.

Alternate Solutions was formally launched in 2011. At that time we were a team of university professors striving to play our part in making a positive impact on the community. We believe that every single individual is vital as change agents. Our work strategy is to connect stakeholders. We have for example been very successful in getting together companies' CSR programs to connect with demand needs for development and promoting entrepreneurship. Similarly we bring corporate leaders to student organizations to enhance their skills and competency. Vocational schools for women have also been established and market linkages have been provided by connecting them to relevant industries.

What were the challenges and what were the opportunities? How did you capitalize on the opportunities and overcome the challenges?

Our biggest challenge was limitation of resources. So we converted this challenge into an opportunity and started working with our students to do a lot of community work through volunteerism. Similarly with Kauffman's program we had the same limitation as we were not funded or sponsored. But through sheer hard work, motivation and creative utilization of human resources we have been able to make GEW-Pakistan a big brand when it comes to entrepreneurship and its promotion. Today our main sponsors and supporters are from the U.S. embassy that is promoting efforts to increase entrepreneurship.

How did you connect with foreign partners and who do you partner with generally?

Through the platform of Global Entrepreneurship Week-Pakistan we are connected to 140 countries. GEW-Pakistan is working closely with U.S. Embassy Islamabad and GEW Global USA to initiate a regional conference on entrepreneurship. We are also in direct talks with all our partners to show an expression of interest in such an initiative. We partner with CIPE (Center for International Private Enterprise), the U.S. embassy, UNIDO, (United Nations Industrial Development Organization) the chambers of commerce and industry in Islamabad, Lahore, Karachi, and Peshawar, the Higher Education Commission of Pakistan, various local universities, Plan9 of the Punjab Information Technology Board and Aman Foundation. All these organizations have signed memorandums of understanding (MoUs) with Alternate Solutions. These organizations help in promoting entrepreneurship by providing guest speaker sessions, workshops, and conferences. They also share their resources and provide their platform to share information to the general public at large.

How did you grow? What are you products now? How are you planning on expanding/diversifying your products?

Our model of partnership is fairly simple. Anyone who is interested in promoting entrepreneurship can become our partner and has to perform one activity. This simple exercise has grown into a movement. Our featured products are 10 international competitions that are now available for all Pakistanis to participate. From this year we will start GEW-Top10 in which we will celebrate and award Pakistan's top 10. GEW-Pakistan also intends to develop Facebook pages for all the cities of Pakistan to promote their local artists, craftsman, women entrepreneurs, manufacturers, and producers. They will be later connected to online portals for promoting and selling their products.

How is your product unique? Why does it have a competitive advantage?

In entrepreneurship our core strength is outreach and connectivity. If you look at our partners we cover the whole length and breadth of the country. We have a good reputation and our work requires us to promote entrepreneurship at all levels. Our organization unlike other organizations in this space is not limited to a city. Therefore we can operate with less hierarchy and more flexibility. This gives us an edge over our existing competitors and therefore we can make a strong impact in the community.

Given your business and sector, where do you see the market going? What opportunities are there for collaboration with large and medium entrepreneurs in the United States?

Technology transfers can be the first and foremost area. Then there is a lot of potential for B2B [business to business] businesses and mobile commerce, franchise businesses, IT, and application development businesses. Another area of potential in the future is going to be green technology in Pakistan.

Can you give details of startups that have won in national and international competitions for innovation?

Go-Fig Solutions, the winner of Pakistan StartUp Cup, has won the first ever World StartUp Cup as well. StartUp Cup is a global network of 68 accelerators "without walls" featuring business model competitions in more than 57 countries.

Go-Fig Solutions was competing with six other teams selected from around the globe. These teams included winners of local StartUp Cups from Egypt, Malaysia, Russia, Philippines, Lebanon, and Ghana. World StartUp Cup was held in Yeveran, Armenia, and was created to recognize and celebrate the achievements of outstanding entrepreneurs who were able to win their local StartUp Cup competitions. Winners from over 21 StartUp Cups from around the globe competed for the final seven positions to present their business plans to the panel of judges at the World StartUp Cup. The 21 winners of the local competition competed virtually for the final seven spots, the selected entrepreneurs presented their business models to an international panel of judges which comprised of local StartUp Cups from around the world.

Go-Fig Solutions are dedicated to identifying issues and coming up with ICT-based solutions. Their process involves taking up a problem, defining it, rigorously research[ing] the key components, present[ing] it to public through trainings and consulting, publishing scholarly and mainstream articles about the problem, and then offering ICT-oriented tools to solve the issue.

Another example is XGear, which was one of the three finalists of Startup Open,[8] led by Ahmed Khalid who has written a book on protocol optimization for Wireless Sensor Networks and a car enthusiast.

Cars produce a lot of data which can be used to improve the driving experience. Unlike XGear, most of the current applications require a large amount of human intervention. XGear opens countless possibilities to the developer community by giving access to the API (application programmable interface) to develop amazing apps. "For example, with XGear, you become aware of your environment and the effects it has on your car's performance, the car then speaks to you and driving becomes a whole new experience. XGear transports engine data onto an easy-to-read screen. Data becomes information explaining how you can drive, maintain and manage your car better. Data is no longer wasted but is now information making sense."[9]

Information Communications and Technologies

CASE STUDY: PERSONFORCE

Personforce is a job site that caters to a niche market—colleges and media blogs—in the United States. The back end operations such as software development, research, and technical support are undertaken in Islamabad, Pakistan.

Atif Mumtaz, cofounder, Personforce

How and why did you start your business in 2006? What was your core product?

The company was established in 2006 in Silicon Valley. We consider it as a Silicon Valley startup right out of Stanford. The founders of Personforce are Rohin Dhar and Atif Mumtaz.

---

8. Startup Open is part of the Global Entrepreneurship Week and recognizes and rewards the entrepreneurs behind successful startups.

9. XGear, "XGear—The game changer for automotive industry," http://www.onestepsolutions.biz/XGear/.

It was started as a provider of niche job boards in the Silicon Valley for colleges and for media blogs. Over 5,000 employers have posted jobs on our system and over a hundred publishers use our job board.

What were the challenges and what were the opportunities? How did you capitalize on the opportunities and overcome the challenges?

The online HR market is crowded in the United States. Monster, Dice, LinkedIn, and similar job boards are megaliths dwarfing out the competition. Therefore, we had to think innovatively. Instead of being a generic job board covering the whole continent of North America, we chose to focus on a niche market—the Silicon Valley tech sector. There, as well, we chose to focus on providing a job board solution to top media blogs and colleges rather than selling directly to the employers. Over time, we were able to corner this market and are now considered one of the three major providers of job board software in our category.

What could you not capitalize on? And has this changed?

There are many ifs and buts of what we could have done. But, we believe, given the circumstances, we have done the best we could.

How did you connect with foreign partners?

The best way to connect with foreign partners is to be there. We chose to have presence in Silicon Valley so that we are just a phone call away.

How did you grow? What are you products now? How are you planning on expanding/diversifying your products?

We grew by signing up more and more customers. We also signed up some of the premium customers in our market. Publishers include companies like TechCrunch, Stanford, MIT, and Harvard college newspapers. Employers that post jobs with us include Apple, Google, Yahoo, Amazon, and other similar companies.

Where do you see the market going? What opportunities are there for collaboration with large and medium entrepreneurs in the United States?

It is an exciting time for the HR market in the United States. LinkedIn, Facebook, and social networks have changed the way recruitment is done in the United States. Therefore, plain vanilla job boards have difficulty in surviving. Monster is already feeling the heat. Dice and others will also not survive if they do not change.

Working with large and medium U.S. enterprises will help us grow outside the United States with social recruitment focus. European, Russian, and Far East markets are ripe for exploitation and we can do just that if we can create a huge impact with our technology and brand name.

How have you used your learning for promoting entrepreneurship or engaging in entrepreneur activities in Pakistan?

I manage the back end operations of this enterprise in Islamabad, where all the software development, technical support, and research and development takes place, while sales and client relationship management activities [occur] in the United States.

In addition, I also run a rural health program in Northern Pakistan. Since 2008, over 200,000 patients have been treated who live below the poverty line. At the same time, I was instrumental in developing a Tele-health application that is used to track diseases, patient demographics, and manage rural health workers activities. This application won the best mHealth application in South Asia (mBillionth Award, 2010) beating out competitors from all across the world. It has also attracted funding from USAID, Google, ISIF (Information Society Innovation Fund) Asia, and government of Pakistan.

Prior to Personforce, I founded Pakistan's first online recruitment portal, called Bright-Spyre in 2002. The portal is considered instrumental in jumpstarting Internet business in Pakistan (TED 2009) and was able to get all major enterprises off the traditional newspaper advertisements onto online recruitment.

Are there legal and administrative barriers that can easily be overcome?

There are always barriers and issues. But entrepreneurs find a way through or around them. For now, there is nothing that cannot be overcome.

CASE STUDY: CREATIVE CHAOS

Creative Chaos is a software development company that develops customer specific software, and web and mobile applications globally.

Shakir Husain, founder and CEO, Creative Chaos

How and why did you start your business? What was your core product?

I started the business in August 2000. Conventional wisdom suggested that starting a software company in Pakistan that year was a terrible idea given the recent tech crash in the United States starting in March 2000. Creative Chaos was founded as a software company offering custom development solutions [for] customers. Fourteen years later this is still our sweet spot.

What were the challenges and what were the opportunities? How did you capitalize on the opportunities and overcome the challenges?

As a first generation entrepreneur there were lots of challenges but the opportunity was that a lot of overseas customers were looking for software services but couldn't afford to get them onshore. Having worked in the private equity industry, I had a lot of relationships which I leveraged to get work in so the "sales" side of things worked well. The challenges ranged from simple business issues to strikes to power cuts and managing human resources. I was fortunate enough to have a very supportive network, whether it was my family or friends, who offered advice and assistance whenever required. I was also lucky enough to have mentors who I could turn to for advice and insights. There is the theory of entrepreneurship and then there's the real world—like any other industry, the gap between them is far and wide.

What could you not capitalize on? And has this changed?

There were quite a few opportunities which we couldn't capitalize on because of lack of capital and there was no avenue to turn to, whether it was the banks and at that time there were a couple of VCs [venture capital firms] which had started [as a result of] Shaukat Aziz's capital market reforms. Unfortunately, access to capital hasn't changed much for entrepreneurs in Pakistan. The silver lining is that there are some accelerator programs, some incubators, and a lot more angel investors. The bad news is that until the State Bank of Pakistan gets banks to start lending to entrepreneurs, nothing is going to change. Pakistan still remains steeped in a culture of rent-seeking with zero incentive to anyone helping to finance a business. However, market forces and new players entering the market and forcing competition are also driving positive changes in the regulatory environment, financial markets, and generally ease of doing business.

How did you connect with foreign partners?

I leveraged my professional and personal network to connect with overseas partners and customers.

How did you grow? What are you products now? How are you planning on expanding/ diversifying your products?

We've grown tremendously and it's all been because of a great team and being able to deliver a quality service. Our customers have been our best sales tool with referrals to new clients and recommending us to whoever needs our services. Over the last few years we've restructured and now have different business units focusing on different solutions. Each unit has separate leadership and management and they're responsible for the targets set. The core at Creative Chaos still remains custom, though we have a company which specializes in payments, one that is the largest digital agency in Pakistan, and another which works with telecoms across the region. Technology is a space where you constantly need to be evolving and innovating so the subsidiaries will just keep increasing.

Where do you see the market going? What opportunities are there for collaboration with large and medium entrepreneurs in the United States?

We feel that the opportunities for growth are infinite. Consider this: a software engineer in Silicon Valley three years out of undergrad commands 175k [US$175,000] as a minimum salary—and that doesn't include loaded cost like insurance to the employer. That combined with the fact that we have world class engineers who can compete with anyone anywhere makes it quite a combination. Currently, we work with Fortune 500 companies, startups on the east coast and the valley, and some of the best names in the technology industry. There's no reason why we can't grow even more.

Generally in the economy, where are the opportunities for growth and international investment?

Pakistan's economy is full of opportunities for anyone who's willing to put in the time and effort to look. I can't think of a single sector which isn't capable of great returns for investors. And for all the doom and gloom talk around the economy all the foreign players which have invested in Pakistan have done extremely well (mining perhaps being an exception with the recent setbacks). Whenever we've had business partners come and visit us in Pakistan (and yes they still come), they've been blown away by what they see and experience.

Pakistan's biggest problem is our government and our bureaucracy. The government has taken it on themselves to bring investment to Pakistan, yet the very people trying to do this do not understand how business, marketing, or PR [public relations] work. It's a joke. Imagine having an awesome world class product but the worst imaginable marketing team in the world. That's what Pakistan is like.

Are there legal and administrative barriers that can easily be overcome?

All of them can be easily overcome. All we need is competence, imagination, and political will. I'm not holding my breath for any, but I'm completely bullish on Pakistan and our investments and work will be here for years to come.

CASE STUDY: NAYATEL

Wahaj-us-Siraj, cofounder and CEO, Nayatel

How and why did you start your business? What was your core product?

Nayatel is Pakistan's first company to provide first fiber to the home (FTTH) services. This includes, but is not limited to, broadband Internet, cable TV, and telephony for home customers and corporate point to point data.[10]

The first business venture was a small PC [personal computer] hardware shop in Islamabad in 1997–98 with one cofounder working full time and one tea boy. The other cofounder used to work in the evenings after his office work and assemble the personal computers. In 1998, a small dial-up Internet service provider business was started in Taxila, a small town an hour's drive from Islamabad, because the area did not have Internet access at that time. The company, called Micronet, grew to seven team members. In 2002, the groups launched Pakistan's first broadband service using digital subscriber line (DSL) technology with a team of 20 members, known as Micronet Broadband. The team then launched Pakistan's first fiber to the home (FTTH) service in 2006 in Islamabad and Rawalpindi and since then has been [on a] steady growth path with 730 strong team members in 2014.

What were the challenges and what were the opportunities? How did you capitalize on the opportunities and overcome the challenges?

When we started the business, we had very little capital. There was an opportunity to provide better product and after sales services to the customers than what was currently being provided to customers. This was the opportunity. The challenge was availability of money. One cofounder sold his small car, another sold his personal computer, and the third contributed Rs 100,000 in cash. So the total cash was around Rs 350,000. But we managed to get computer supplies from a shop in Lahore on credit.

Who do you partner with and why?

The three cofounders were friends from university. They shared the same ideology and values. The common purpose for starting a business together was to make money by using legitimate means. The initial shareholders were friends with whom the cofounders had done initial business and the shareholders invested their money because they thought they could trust the integrity and competence of the founders.

---

10. For more information, see Nayatel, "Services we offer," www.nayatel.com.

How did you grow? What are you products now? How are you planning on expanding/diversifying your products?

The growth in optical fiber network is all about designing a good network, and then its execution. Of course, availability of capital remains a big challenge as the business is capital extensive. The vision of Nayatel is to become Pakistan's number one FTTH company covering all major cities with a brand new and future proof network having a life of 20 to 30 years.

How is your product unique? Why does it have a competitive advantage?

No other operator in Pakistan is providing FTTH service. That makes Nayatel's product unique. The customer orientation of Nayatel is top rated. Nayatel has a rich portfolio of services that include broadband Internet, cable TV, and telephony for home customers and point to point data, corporate telephony for business customers. In the cable TV market, Nayatel is the only operator in Pakistan providing high definition (HD) cable TV and video on demand.

Given your business and sector, where do you see the market going? What opportunities are there for collaboration with large and medium entrepreneurs in the United States?

The demand of bandwidth by the businesses and home consumers has been on the rise. Most cities of Pakistan are currently without reliable optical fiber last mile networks that can deliver high bandwidth connections for ever increasing demand of cable TV including high definition TV and video. As telecom revenues shrink globally, revenues of entertainment and TV services are growing. Nayatel is strongly positioned to take advantage of this shift as the Pakistani cable TV market gradually transforms to digital and then to HD with analog cable TV service providers gradually disappearing from the market. U.S. entrepreneurs willing to invest in Pakistan can team with local entrepreneurs to expand such businesses.

CASE STUDY: VISTECH SOLUTIONS

VisTech Solutions provides customer specific mobile and web applications to customers in Pakistan and the United States to support business management services and leverage information technology to provide cost-effective solutions for customers.[11]

Barkan Saeed, founder and CEO, VisTech Solutions, interview

How and why did you start your business in 2007?

After graduating in 2006, I worked for a year and a half at a company in Islamabad. I realized that I could start my own business. I left the job and hired two software engineers

---

11. For more information, see VisTech Solutions, "Welcome to our Company," www.vistechgroup.com.

and rented a small apartment. I had no fear of failing which helped me a lot to take the risk of leaving my job, hiring people from my savings, and starting the business. VisTech Solutions is an IT solutions provider providing mobile and web applications

What were the challenges and what were the opportunities? How did you capitalize on the opportunities and overcome the challenges?

Since I had no experience as a manager or any education on how to manage a business, I faced a lot of difficulties in the beginning related to managing people, and sales. The biggest challenge during the business was how to develop processes in the business so that dependence on myself was reduced and how to deliver on time and quality along with exponential growth. We overcame those challenges by focusing on the key problems that we were having and then experimentation on different solutions that we tried.

We did have some good opportunities along the way. We worked on some great products that are now making millions of dollars per year for our clients. We capitalized on the success of those products and referrals to get more business.

There were many opportunities along the way where we could have gotten equity on the projects we worked on or being part of the products that came to us. I think we are capitalizing on that well now by being partners in most solutions that we develop and also the opportunities in the product space.

How did you connect with foreign partners?

For the initial six years, we mostly connected with clients through Elance and oDesk.[12] Some of the good clients came as referrals from our friends and in the past few years, visits to U.S. [the United States] and Dubai have also helped us connect with clients and partners abroad.

How did you grow?

There were a couple of factors that can be attributed to our growth:

- Delivering quality to our initial customers who referred us to other good customers.

- By creating a process that allowed us to manage large teams that helped us keep the quality of our projects along with growth.

---

12. Elance and oDesk are job sites to hire people who freelance. See Elance, "Hire a talented Freelancer," https://www.elance.com/p/lpg/freelancing/?rid=1TN5N&utm_source=google&utm_medium=cpc&utm_campaign=C-Brand-Exact&utm_term=elance&utm_content=f1&ad=42114818418&bmt=e&adpos=1t1&gclid=CjwKEAjwiumdBRDZyvKvqb_6mkUSJABDyYOzg79eGiBo2eRwIYd-i2iulCwdSwTnTdBqXqJIGiPowRoC-17w_wcB; and oDesk, "Get more done . . . with the help of a freelancer," https://www.odesk.com.

Where do you see the market going? What opportunities are there for collaboration with large and medium entrepreneurs in the United States?

I see a huge potential in the ICT sector for Pakistan. Pakistan has, in the past, had an image issue. However, anyone who has worked with us in the past has stayed with us. I believe this initial barrier can be overcome by sharing Pakistani success stories. The image recently has also been improved by continuation of democracy and a business friendly government in Islamabad.

If we develop strong partnerships with entrepreneurs in the United States, I believe it could be a win-win situation for both the parties as other countries—especially the ones famous for ICT like India and the Ukraine—are heating up and these companies will soon need new partners. Pakistan, with its resource pool, is an excellent next destination for growth for these companies.

Fast-Moving Consumer Goods

CASE STUDY: NATIONAL FOODS

National Foods began as a spice company to make food that is hygienic, reduce time spent in the kitchen by women, foster health, and cater to individual needs and convenience. National Foods provides different products with the objective of providing convenience and quick preparation of foods to cater to the growing market in Pakistan as well as globally.[13]

Abrar Hasan, CEO, National Foods, interview

Why and when was your business started?

The business was started in 1970 by the acquisition of a food product development laboratory. The business model was converted to a manufacturing model in extension to the product development lab, which still is the nucleus of business today. The company's focal point still remains on customer's needs through product development in line with the changing market trends.[14]

What were some of the challenges and opportunities you faced?

The challenges were to establish a food brand in Pakistan in the 1970s, especially in a market that was not used to branding and depended on informal practices in a highly fragmented market. The challenges also were to make consumers accept food in packaging

---

13. For more information on National Foods and its products and services, see www.nfoods.com.
14. Nasir, "100 business leaders, entrepreneurs and difference makers of Pakistan." Additional information added for clarity.

as opposed to the lifestyle of procuring spices from wholesalers and grinding it in front of them, thus creating a perception of quality and freshness as opposed to convenience. The company overcame these challenges by having a focused brand positioning on hygiene, quality, and convenience which became the guiding ethos. The next challenge was national distribution within Pakistan and slowly the brand was cemented through effective distribution covering the whole country. The opportunities [to] date are conversion of the category map from unbranded consumption to branded consumption which is an ongoing quest to capitalize the potential.

Has National Foods won any accolades/awards?

The National brand was ranked as #2 out of 3,500 brands in Pakistan through a market research study conducted four years ago. It was between two brands of Unilever, a leading multinational company, so it was a huge achievement.

How can U.S. investment or co-ventures benefit/help this market segment?

The food market is moving toward convenience through ready-to-consume products. Lifestyles are changing very rapidly and with women adopting careers at an increasing rate it is giving rise to convenience-based products. Collaboration with U.S. companies in this segment can yield high growth opportunities.

Where do you think there is potential for American investment?

Pakistan is a sizable consumer market with a population around 200 million. The market is still largely untapped with the non-branded consumption far outweighing the branded consumption. Investment in ready-to-consume branded food products will create enhanced brand penetrations with good margins, thus paving way for good growth. The typical growth rates for branded food products are within 15 to 25 percent annually. The total food market each year grows by approximately 10 percent. This is a great opportunity for investors to look into partnering with local established players for effective capitalization of this opportunity. Also as Pakistan is a developing nation, poverty and malnutrition are at a very high rate. The past few years, there have been natural calamities in the shape of floods, droughts, and earthquakes which further exacerbates the situation. Opportunity of high-nutrition meals for infants and children in disaster-affected areas is a huge opportunity that can be tapped through the government working in alleviating the problems of malnutrition.

Pharmaceutical Industry

CASE STUDY: MEDIPAK LIMITED

Nasir J. Chowdhry, managing director, Medipak Limited

How and why did you start your business? What was your core product?

Medipak was established in 1986 to help meet a gap in the market for locally produced pharmaceutical products. Our core product was parenteral solutions (IV [intravenous] solutions).

What were the challenges and what were the opportunities? How did you capitalize on the opportunities and overcome the challenges? What could you not capitalize on? And has this changed?

At the time of our inception there were no local manufacturing facilities in the country. We faced challenges in laying the groundwork for our business and in educating the public about our products. These challenges, however, also allowed us to capitalize on the gap in the market and facilitated our entry. We were able to establish ourselves as the first company to introduce foreign technology and lifesaving infusion solutions and distinguished ourselves with our consistent quality and strong marketing.

We were not able to expand at a vigorous pace as most of our efforts were concentrated on strengthening our core product. Today our infusion solutions are well established and we are expanding into other products.

How did you connect with foreign partners?

We connected with foreign parties in pursuit of technology transfer. In our efforts we identified key companies with competency in IV solution manufacturing. At the time Germany, France, Japan, Italian, and U.S. companies were the industry leaders. We chose to collaborate (and continue to do so) with a German company, Fresenius.

How did you grow? What are you products now? How are you planning on expanding/diversifying your products?

We grew by expanding into several different lines of production which include infusion solutions, infusion administration sets, ophthalmic products, solid dosage products, dialysis and irrigation solutions, medical disposable, imported, injectable, and oncology products.

Medipak Limited signed an agreement with Chinese company Hunan China Sun in May 2013 to double our production capacity by constructing a new IV solution plant. We believe in strengthening our core IV solution product while extensively expanding in other areas.

Where do you see the market going? What opportunities are there for collaboration with large and medium entrepreneurs in the United States?

We see a marked shift in the industry toward biotechnology and its derivative products, particularly vaccines. The opportunities for collaboration are abundant as local companies require technological know-how that can be provided by U.S. companies looking to expand into the South Asian region.

Generally, where are the opportunities for growth and international investment in your sector? Are there legal and administrative barriers that can easily be overcome?

The pharmaceutical industry is perhaps Pakistan's most dynamic sector as it caters directly to our ever increasing population. There are very few legal and administrative barriers to entry in Pakistan. In fact, we have one of the most accessible economies in the region with a strong investor friendly atmosphere and numerous incentives. Unfortunately foreign investment has decreased due to a turbulent law-and-order situation in the country.

Why do you think the pharmaceutical industry is a competitive one, where American investments could also have a comparative advantage?

Local companies are looking toward biotechnology and specialized products and their manufacture needs international support from companies with technological knowledge. This increasing trend provides a perfect climate for U.S. investment in a largely formulation-based industry. Most companies import chemicals and packaging from abroad and international investment can help change that.

Low-Cost Private Education

CASE STUDY: AMERICAN SCHOOL OF INTERNATIONAL ACADEMICS (ASIA)

ASIA schools provide education based on the American curriculum, and also includes the Pakistani national requirements of curriculum such as religious studies for students including those with special needs. The curriculum is highly innovative and uses the latest IT solutions and research to give students a competitive advantage.[15]

---

15. For more information about the ASIA schools, see www.asiaschools.pk.edu.

Ayesha Hamid, founder and CEO, ASIA

How and why did you start ASIA? What was your core product?

I am running an American School [of International Academics] as a "Pvt. Ltd." incorporated in Nevada but functioning in Pakistan. The schools curriculum is based on the U.S. system of schooling. I have the required U.S. credentials to run and operate this business anywhere in the world. My expertise to run an[this] American School comes from my education in New York City, and the [experiences with other] overseas American Schools, and the required Accreditation to run a school based on American curriculum.

In Pakistan, there is a need for quality education in English. There was also no help for special needs students and no place for them in schools. ASIA became a model school for the inclusion or mainstream of special needs students in regular schools. ASIA was the first low-cost American curriculum school in Pakistan where students got a chance to be prepared for college and university.

What were the challenges and what were the opportunities? How did you capitalize on the opportunities and overcome the challenges?

The challenges I faced were the government bureaucracy, lack of clear rules and regulations, and anti-American sentiment. I worked diligently and consistently to convince the education ministry to recognize ASIA and its diploma and equate it to the local system so that students who could not go abroad could get into the top local institutions. I formed a pressure group with the help of parents and like-minded people to make rules for such schools in the private sector. I capitalized on these challenges and strengthened the system so strongly that I was able to create my own niche. The key to my success was my strong knowledge base which was helpful in negotiations with all for recognition and a legal status, given that I had a diploma in education from the United States.

What have been your successes?

My students have gone to great institutions all over the world and are today doctors, engineers, pilots, army men, bureaucrats, ministers, businessmen, teachers, and CEOs of MNCs [multinational companies] or owners of MNCs.

How is your product unique? Why does it have a competitive advantage?

It is [a] unique school with strong vision and characteristics that offers students a lifelong plan for their future careers, from preschool to university and beyond. We also now do job placements and business entrepreneurial activities. No other school in the entire country of Pakistan, especially in the private sector, has the charter and accreditation that we have, and we provide special needs services as an inclusive program.

Given your business and sector, where do you see the market going? What opportunities are there for collaboration with large and medium entrepreneurs in the United States?

There are tremendous opportunities for growth in the educational sector through collaborations with U.S. colleges and universities as the need for good quality, yet affordable, education is growing in Pakistan.

Is it easy to do business in Pakistan?

There is extreme ease of business but you need to have the right kind of partners for investment, people who know it all and have done it the right way. The law will give tremendous protection to the investor as it did to me.

High-End Retail Franchises

CASE STUDY: DYNASTY LTD.

Dynasty Ltd. caters to the high-end watch market in Pakistan and has the franchise for Rado.

Rumman Ahmed, CEO, Dynasty Ltd., interview

How was your business started?

The business was started by my father in 1992. He used to work as the Rado[16] agent at that time. The agency was terminated in 1988–1989 and for a few years Rado did not have an official agent. When they decided to re-enter the Pakistani market, they invited proposals from various people, and among them was my father. He was selected and started business in late 1992. I joined in September 1993 after working in a bank for three years.

What were the challenges and what were the opportunities? How did you capitalize on the opportunities and overcome the challenges?

The opportunities at the time were for a business that was run professionally and in line with international standards and requirements. We capitalized on a fragmented market with no price structure, which also suffered from competition of smuggled goods for high-value watches. At that time, retail-oriented outlets were not willing to expand into distribution and preferred to be the primary source.[17] We capitalized on this and were able to create a niche where we were able to distribute freely without competition in distribution. With time, we grew and managed countrywide distribution, providing us

---

16. Rado is a watch company.
17. Retailers were willing to take on distribution, but due to their way of doing business at that time, it meant getting a sale at any cost even if undercutting their own dealers—not a very successful model.

with a comparative advantage for other high-value watch brands, and also other brands in general because of our quality-focused model.

Pricing was the biggest challenge in the market at the time. Since we were importing goods our prices were more expensive than smuggled goods and different dealers charged different prices depending on their negotiation skills and needs. My first job was to set up a fair price structure that was also communicated to all our vendors with no exceptions. We were successful in aligning our interests and objectives with all retailers and distribution outlets. To counter the issue of low-cost smuggled goods, we negotiated with the principals to lower the ex-factory price for us, and then established a pricing policy that was based on the prevailing price in Dubai rather than on our cost. This policy did sacrifice our margins, but it also ensured that we got more volume in our business, since smuggling was not very profitable for the gray market operators. The factory also cooperated with us by installing serial numbers on their watches which could be traced back to the source. So if smuggled watches were found in our market we sent the serial numbers back and they took action against the party responsible.

What could you not capitalize on? And has this changed?

During the 1990s there were a lot of brands looking for agents in Pakistan, but we had to refuse them due to limited resources. These brands then appointed other players as agents, but we are still on top with almost 50 percent of imports by value. We have now started looking for new brands to add to our portfolio. Some of the higher end-retailers have entered the market but Rado and Tisso are still on top.

The jewel in the crown for all the owners of the company has been our appearance at number 87 in the ranking of top taxpayers in Pakistan (the partnership sector). We believe this is a vindication of our efforts of 20 years to operate cleanly and a belief that one can earn money doing a fully legal business. We are perhaps one of two in the industry who import all products 100 percent and at full invoice value. We have been recognized by the tax authorities as being above board, and have heard from sources that even our competitors are quick to point out that we are honest businessmen.

Where do you see the market going? What opportunities are there for collaboration with large and medium entrepreneurs in the United States?

I see the market in general in very bullish terms. I think Pakistan is at the cusp of explosive growth in the economy. It has a large population, consumer demand, and the natural resources for companies to take advantage of. What seems to be holding the country back is a poor image and lack of security. For everything else, including corruption and poor leadership, I believe that market forces will act to set things right. However, progress on the security side will result in exponential positive spillovers.

Regarding collaboration with U.S. entrepreneurs, personally I believe that the real benefit for the country and the market would be if this collaboration brings in systems, procedures, management methods, innovation techniques, use of technology, and other such skills in order to truly benefit themselves and the country. As is slowly being proved, having cheap labor is not an indicator of long-term success, but being able to maximize the potential of each unit of labor is what is required. This is the value that the Western businessman can add to the market. Money, of course, is always welcome too!

Generally in the economy, where are the opportunities for growth and international investment?

Given the size of the population, food and FMCGs [fast-moving consumer goods] is the most obvious answer. There are also backward integration opportunities with farming and sales of modern equipment and implements. Training in agriculture to improve yields and investment in growing corporate farming in Pakistan. And finally as a result of the growth of these sectors there will definitely be an expansion of retail, especially in the luxury sector. Entertainment is another industry that has financial potential as well as social implications. There is already a lot of wealth and money available locally that needs to be channeled into viable projects, and American investment can reap returns by partnering with such organizations.

Are there legal and administrative barriers that can easily be overcome?

There certainly are barriers. The red tape is long, and trust is short. So an international investor will have to choose his partner wisely or else he could get tangled in a web. An honest, trustworthy local partner can help overcome barriers and grow a business, albeit slowly. So the investors have to look at a longer time frame.

About the Author

Sadika Hameed is an expert in investment climate and political risk analysis for frontier and emerging markets and a fellow with the CSIS Program on Crisis, Conflict, and Cooperation. She has worked on issues related to security and terrorism in South Asia. Ms. Hameed worked as an economist and governance specialist with the World Bank and the U.S. Agency for International Development in Afghanistan and Pakistan. Her areas of expertise include political risk analysis, gauging investment climates, small and medium enterprise (SME) development, due diligence work, monitoring and evaluation of multilateral programs, economics, security, and governance issues in South Asia and the Middle East. Ms. Hameed earned an M.A. in international policy studies from Stanford University in International Negotiation and Conflict Management, an M.Sc. in economics from the London School of Economics, and a B.A. in economics and finance from the University of Manchester. She has also worked on issues relating to subnational governance structures and business growth, cooperation in South Asia, private-sector development in fragile states, and U.S responses to transitions and potential transitions.